# THE PERFORMANCE OF COMPANIES

# Mitsui Lectures in Economics

*Series Editor*: L. Alan Winters, University of Birmingham

Perfect Markets and Easy Virtue
*William J. Baumol, with Sue Anne Batey Blackman*

The Performance of Companies
*Stephen Nickell*

**Forthcoming**

International Monetary Theory
*Paul R. Krugman*

# The Performance of Companies

## The Relationship between the External Environment, Management Strategies and Corporate Performance

Stephen Nickell

BLACKWELL
Oxford UK & Cambridge USA

First published 1995

Blackwell Publishers, the publishing imprint of
Basil Blackwell Ltd
108 Cowley Road
Oxford OX4 1JF
UK

Basil Blackwell Inc.
238 Main Street
Cambridge, Massachusetts 02142
USA

*British Library Cataloguing in Publication Data*

A CIP catalogue record for this book is available from the British Library.

*Library of Congress Cataloging-in-Publication Data*

Nickell, S. J.
The performance of companies : the relationship between the
external environment, management strategies and corporate
performance / Stephen Nickell.
p.   cm. — (Mitsui lectures in economics)
Includes bibliographical references and index.
ISBN 0–631–19731–1 (alk. paper)
1. Industrial productivity—Measurement.   2. Corporate governance.
3. Strategic planning.   4. Production management.   5. Competition.
I. Title.   II. Series.
HD56.25.N53   1995                                      94–36320
658.4—dc20                                                    CIP

Typeset in 10½ on 13½pt Palatino
by Graphicraft Typesetters Ltd, Hong Kong
Printed in Great Britain by T.J. Press Ltd, Padstow, Cornwall

# Contents

# Acknowledgements

This book emerged from an invitation to deliver the 1992 Mitsui Lectures at the University of Birmingham. I am most grateful to Alan Winters and the University of Birmingham for their hospitality, to the Mitsui Corporation for making these lectures possible and to the Economic and Social Research Council and the Leverhulme Trust for funding this research. The work was carried out under the auspices of the ESRC Centre for Economic Performance, Corporate Performance Programme.

I would like to thank John Vickers for many useful discussions, Maha Mansour, Daphne Nicolitsas and Giovanni Urga for helpful research assistance, and Colin Mayer, Andrew Oswald and Geoffrey Owen for their valuable comments on an earlier draft.

Stephen Nickell

# 1

# The Analysis and Measurement of Corporate Performance

## INTRODUCTION

Why should we be interested in corporate performance? Because the performance of companies is the major driving force behind the wealth of nations. While it is true that everything ultimately comes down to the behaviour and talents of individuals, it is the ability to harness these talents in production which ultimately determines economic performance. And it is the company sector which plays the key role in this regard.

Bearing this in mind, what do we mean by the performance of a company? How can it be measured and, if it can be measured, how should it be analysed? These are the topics of this chapter.

## 1　A Basic Measure of Performance

Some companies perform better than others. This is an indisputable fact, but how do we recognize a high performing company? Does it produce a product which is universally recognized to be outstanding, like a Rolls-Royce motor car? Perhaps not, since the producers of these cars have lost a great deal of money in recent years. Do its shareholders make a lot of money? This is a dangerous criterion because it is so unstable. For example, one thousand pounds invested in Polly Peck in 1979 would have made the investor a millionaire by 1989. Polly Peck was the best performing share on the UK stockmarket in the 1980s. Yet by 1991, the original stake would have been worthless. So, as measures of corporate performance, share prices are tricky to use.

What about profits? Is a very profitable company a high performer? Here, it depends a little on what you mean. For example, British Telecom is very profitable, as are most telephone companies the world over. However, it is often argued that they are not very efficient, don't provide a good service and only make a great deal of money because of their monopoly position in the market. This suggests that we should not judge performance solely by the private gains to the stakeholders in a company. Monopoly power may provide substantial benefits to shareholders and workers alike, but the costs imposed on the rest of us may easily outweigh these gains. So we would like to try and eliminate certain monopoly elements when trying to pin down performance.

For the moment, however, let us leave this point aside and begin with the common-sense notion that a successful company is one that produces a lot of output relative to the inputs it uses up. To compare these things we can simply use their market value, so we start with the difference between the value of what is produced and the value of the inputs required to produce it. If we denote this difference by $\Pi$, then we have

$$\Pi = R - wN - cK - p_m M \tag{1}$$

where $R$ is sales revenue, $N$ is employment, $w$ is wage, $K$ is capital stock, $c$ is cost of capital, $M$ is material inputs, $p_m$ is price of material inputs. We suppose here that the firm uses only three inputs $(N, K, M)$. The cost of capital is the trickiest of the prices to measure, being the price which the firm would have to pay, per period, to rent a unit of capital stock. The overall difference, $\Pi$, is known as the rent or super-normal profit or added value (see Kay, 1993, for the last of these).

This measure, $\Pi$, seems like a good measure of performance but it turns out to have a number of problems. First, it is a flow of income over time. So it may mean different things at different times because of inflation. This can be dealt with by supposing that all the terms are normalized on the retail price index, so it becomes a real rather than a nominal flow. But it also fluctuates. It may be high in one period and low in another. So we would probably wish to average over time. One standard way of doing this is to take the present value of the real income stream, $PV\Pi$. Since it is a real stream, we may discount with the real interest rate, $r$, to obtain

$$PV\Pi_t = \int_t^\infty e^{-r(\tau-t)} [R(\tau) - w(\tau)N(\tau) - c(\tau)K(\tau) - p_m(\tau)M(\tau)] d\tau \tag{2}$$

where $PV\Pi_t$ is the present value of the future $\Pi$ stream at time $t$.

In order to see whether or not this is a good measure of performance, we start by seeing how it relates to the rewards received by the owners of the firm. Suppose the owners are those who, at time $t$, possess all the capital stock, $K_t$. What is the future stream of earnings which they command? This, which we term $E$, is given by

$$E = R - wN - qI - p_mM \qquad (3)$$

where $I$ is gross investment (purchases of new capital goods) and $q$ is the price of new capital goods (in terms of the consumption basket). So the stream of earnings is simply the revenue less the variable cost of production and the expenditure on new capital goods. The present value of this earnings stream, $PVE_t$, is given by

$$PVE_t = \int_t^\infty e^{-r(\tau-t)}[R(\tau) - w(\tau)N(\tau) - q(\tau)I(\tau) \qquad (4)$$
$$- p_m(\tau)M(\tau)]d\tau$$

Then it is easy to show (see appendix) that

$$PVE_t = q_tK_t + PV\Pi_t \qquad (5)$$

So the owners start at time $t$ with capital stock $K_t$ valued at $q_tK_t$. Then the present value of the stream of super-normal profits, $PV\Pi_t$, is the extra present value earnings they can obtain over and above the initial value of the capital stock at replacement cost. This suggests that $PV\Pi_t$ might well be a good measure of company performance.

Suppose, however, that we want to compare different size firms. We could normalize on the initial capital, $q_tK_t$. Then (5) becomes

$$\frac{PVE_t}{q_tK_t} = 1 + \frac{PV\Pi_t}{q_tK_t} \qquad (6)$$

and we might judge firms by the ratio of $PV\Pi_t/q_tK_t$. This would be easy to compute, since $PVE_t$ is the market value of the company, and we could then use (6) to obtain a measure of our desired ratio. So is this a good measure of performance? The answer is no, for at least two reasons.

First, the ratio $PVE/qK$, also known as the average $Q$ ratio (after Tobin), is under the control of the firm and, if it is high, the firm will typically act to reduce it. This it can do by raising investment. Why should it wish to do so? Because if $PVE/qK$ is greater than unity (i.e. $PV\Pi$ is positive), the initial capital creates more present value earnings than it costs. This suggests that the same will be true of an extra unit of capital[1] and so an additional unit will be purchased by the owners. As the process continues, $PVE/qK$ will tend to fall, since investment in the company is probably subject to diminishing marginal returns. So we can hardly use, as a measure of company performance, a ratio $(PVE/qK)$ which any sensible owner is trying to reduce when it gets too high.[2]

The second problem arises from the fact that $PVE$, the market value of the firm, merely reflects the best market guess about future earnings flows. This creates difficulties both because these guesses can be very volatile, as the example of Polly Peck indicates, and because what we really want is a measure of performance *now*, not some market guess as to what is going to happen in ten years' time.

We can get around this last problem by taking a simple average of $\Pi$ over recent years, normalizing on average scale as measured by capital stock or value added. This is the measure favoured by Kay (1993, chapter 2). It does, however, have further serious problems, as we shall see.

## 2 WHY SHOULD FIRMS DIFFER?

Taking some average of super-normal profits or added value $(\Pi)$ as our measure of performance, it is interesting to see how firms might differ in this dimension. If we note that the firm's revenue, $R$, may be written as $pY$ where $p$ is the (real) price of output and $Y$ is real sales, then $\Pi$ can be written

$$\Pi = pY - wN - cK - p_mM. \tag{7}$$

So possible differences in performance can arise from differences in the prices ($p$, $w$, $c$, $p_m$) or the technology (the technological relationship between output, $Y$, and the inputs, $N$, $K$, $M$). Let us look at these in turn.

1 *Differences in the price of output*, p. Suppose two firms produce roughly the same product, using the same technology. One firm may, nevertheless, be able to sell its product for a higher price. Why?

- It has a better reputation. Pure reputation effects can arise even for identical goods. For example, the Anon retail store might sell an Anon cashmere wool sweater identical to a St Michael cashmere wool sweater sold in Marks and Spencer. But, because of the reputation of St Michael products sold in Marks and Spencer, the Anon product must be sold at a lower price in order to compete.
- It advertises heavily. This is related to reputation. The firm may have previously advertised its product heavily, thereby generating a larger number of customers and enabling the firm to sell at a higher price. Of course, if this advertising is continuous, then advertising expenditure will also enter $\Pi$, offsetting the higher price of output.
- It has a higher degree of market power. For example, one of the firms may have access to a protected market, either because it entered earlier or because it previously paid an entry fee either officially or in the form of bribes.

2 *Differences in the wage*, w. Two firms may produce the same product with the same technology, yet one may have to pay a higher wage to its workers. The obvious reason for this is that one firm may be unionized and the other not. In the UK, this would give rise to a wage differential of

between 5 and 10 per cent (see Stewart, 1990), depending on the size of the firm and its position in the product market. Alternatively, one of the firms may simply operate in a higher wage location and be forced to pay more in order to compete in the local labour market.

3 *Differences in the cost of capital, c.* Two firms can be similar in most respects except that one has a lower cost of capital. This might be because it has a superior financial structure or a clever finance director, or because the bank considers it to be a safer bet because it has a lower ratio of debt to assets, for example.

4 *Differences in the price of material and other inputs, $p_m$.* Firms may differ in the quality and price of their inputs, often because some firms invest in relationships with their suppliers which enable them to obtain a better deal in the longer term. Alternatively, some firms may simply exercise monopsony power to obtain low price inputs.

5 *Technology.* Here we are concerned with the relationship between inputs and outputs. Some aspects of technology are, of course, governed by the laws of physics. But this is rarely a binding constraint. Firms, in fact, differ dramatically in the amounts of output which they can obtain from a given volume of inputs even when using the same apparent technology. Reasons for this include the following.

- Effort. In some plants workers and managers simply work harder. Manning ratios may be lower, morale may be higher and so on. These differences may relate to wages, unions and industrial relations practices in general.
- Organization of production. Significant differences include the organization of maintenance, the flexibility of the workforce (in terms of the tasks they can or will undertake) and the detection of faulty workmanship. A glance at the work of Sig Prais and his team at the

National Institute (see, for example, Prais and Wagner, 1988; Steedman and Wagner, 1987) reveals how important these factors are in explaining differences in performance.

- The use of innovations. Firms differ in their production and use of product or process innovations. Both enable firms effectively to produce more with given inputs.

So there are innumerable ways in which firms may have different levels of performance on the basis of the $\Pi$ measure. But, in order for these differences to become significant, they must be sustained over time. If firm A does something to improve its productivity, for example, by introducing a superior technology, firm B may be able simply to follow suit and obtain the same improvement. So it is clear that sustained superior performance means that a firm has something which others find hard to copy. This may be because it is a secret (like the recipe for Coca-Cola) but, generally, it is not a secret, merely hard to copy. Kay (1993) uses the example of Liverpool Football Club, which dominated English soccer for over 20 years.[3] Yet its success was very hard to emulate, even by clubs with equivalent resources, such as Manchester United or Arsenal.

Kay (1993) allocates the fundamental sources of superior performance under four headings, *innovation*, *reputation*, *architecture* and *strategic assets*. The notion of innovation is clear and refers to new goods and services, new technologies or simply new ways of doing things. Firms may produce innovations themselves, by using the research and development (R and D) process, for example, or they may copy others. Of course, if innovations can easily be copied, sustained relative improvements in performance are not readily available from this source. However, there may be barriers to the replication of innovations, either legal, as in the form of patent protection, or by simply keeping things secret.

Reputation is harder to copy, because it can only be built up over time and typically requires the expenditure of resources on advertising, for example, or on quality control and the like. An important point, to which we shall return, is the fact that building up a reputation is a form of investment which is typically unmeasured. The consequent existence of unmeasured 'reputation capital' may serve to distort the measurement of super-normal profits or added value, and this may cause serious problems in inter-firm comparisons of performance.

Architecture refers to the structure of the relationships between the firm and its suppliers, employees, bankers and so on. These relationships may be made explicit in the form of written contracts but, more often than not, the contracts are implicit. This makes them harder to replicate and even to describe. So the notion of architecture covers a wide variety of phenomena and, because of this, is perhaps the least satisfactory of Kay's categories. Strategic assets, on the other hand, is a precise concept, covering contracts which are exclusive to a particular firm or group of firms. Examples include duty-free shops at airports, motorway services, car dealerships, salt monopolies, radio or TV networks and so on. More generally, strategic assets might cover the situation where the market does not readily accommodate more than one firm and thus the encumbent has a very strong advantage.

This completes our summary of the sources of performance differences and much of the rest of the book will be devoted to these issues. Next we look at the problems associated with the measurement of differences in corporate performance.

## 3 PROBLEMS OF MEASUREMENT

A major problem with analysing corporate performance is accurately measuring it. We have so far concluded that a sensible measure would be some suitably normalized average of super-normal profit or added value over the recent past (for a good example, see tables 2.4 and 2.5 in Kay, 1993). But this measure is subject to serious practical difficulties, the most important being the unmeasured capital problem.

### Unmeasured investment and capital stock

In order to measure performance, we must account for a firm's stock of capital in the broadest sense of the word. Unfortunately, capital comes in many forms other than buildings, plant, machinery and vehicles. The following is a list of different investments which generate capital that is either unmeasured or not measured with any significant accuracy. Thus the company may

*   make the workforce more productive (accumulate specific human capital) by investing in training;
*   raise the reputation of a product by investing in quality control;
*   make the product more desirable by investing in advertising and promotions;
*   generate new or improved products by investing in R and D;
*   improve the organization of production by investing in human resource management;
*   reduce competition by investing in lobbying (for protectionism, for example).

The optimal strategy for the firm will be to accumulate 'capital' in its various forms until its marginal return falls to the cost of capital. Our inability to observe either the 'capital' or, in most cases, the separate investment expenditures will cause severe difficulties in comparing the true performance of difference companies. For example, consider two firms, A and B, in the same sector, each of which has been going for a long time. Suppose, over this period, firm A has devoted some of its labour input to ensuring that its product is very reliable (by extensive checking etc.) and that firm B has not. So, over the years, firm A has developed a reputation for reliability and hence can sell its product at a considerably higher price than firm B. As a consequence, the current value of firm A's output exceeds the apparent value of its inputs, including the extra labour devoted to checking, by more than that of firm B. Does this mean that firm A is a higher performer than firm B? The person in the street and even the stockmarket analyst would undoubtedly say yes. But this is not clear. In the earlier years, while firm A was building its reputation, its output would not have carried a price premium, because its reputation of reliability was not yet in place. During this period firm A would 'perform' less well than firm B because of the additional labour devoted to quality checking. These extra labour costs were, of course, an investment devoted to building up 'reputation capital'. To take account of this, the true current inputs for firm A should include this 'reputation capital' valued at the cost of capital. If the output price premium enables firm A to increase the value of sales by consistently more that the extra input cost imputed to 'reputation capital', then it is indeed a higher performer than firm B. The investment in reputation was a good one whose average return exceeded its opportunity cost. But this need not be so. Firm A may have significantly over-invested in reputation, for example, but it would still appear to be the better performer on standard measurements. However, firm B might, in fact, have been the higher performing company.

Similar arguments can be adduced for any unmeasured elements of capital. The consequence is that we might be able to say, for example, that firm A has a higher stream of measured super-normal profit or added value than firm B because of its higher past expenditures on R and D or advertising or specific training or quality control. However, using Kay's terminology, firm A's superior reputation or superior innovation performance or superior architecture may simply be the result of past investment expenditures which generate capital that is not properly measured on the balance sheet. So we might then 'explain' the apparent difference in measured performance by these characteristics, but none of this would necessarily mean, for example, that the stakeholders in firm A have had a higher stream of returns *over the long run* than those in the 'inferior' firm B. Indeed, the present value of added value per unit of initial capital over the whole life time of firm A may well be lower than that for firm B.

This problem is widespread. For most companies a part of their current earnings reflects returns to investment expenditures made decades earlier, and we have no current measures of capital corresponding to these expenditures. This suggests that we must consider averages or present values of super-normal profits or added value over very long periods indeed, thereby capturing the early investment expenditures as labour costs, for example.[4] The problem with this, however, is that firms may change their performance. Many companies are seen as high performers in one decade but low performers in another, so we simply cannot take performance measures over very long periods without losing much of the variation of interest.

Thus we have a serious difficulty when it comes to comparing the performance of different companies, which is very hard to overcome if we want to construct performance league tables. However, the role of a performance league table is not simply to identify the top performers, it is to try and ascertain what external factors or internal strategic decisions generate higher performance. Luckily, we can do this without constructing league tables. The basic problem we have identified is that important elements of capital are simply not measured. This is, in fact, part of the wider problem that many factors influencing performance are not measured. However, many of these unmeasured factors are relatively stable over short periods of time. So if we look at a particular firm and we are interested in the impact of some observed external factor or internal strategy on performance, then instead of correlating this factor with performance across companies, we should find a period during which this external factor or internal strategy changes, and compare the performance of the company before and after the change. As long as our unmeasured elements of capital are relatively stable over the relevant period, we shall draw the correct inferences without ever having to measure performance accurately.

This discussion suggests that a time-series or longitudinal approach to analysing company performance will be more reliable than a cross-section approach. Does this mean that cross-sectional analysis is not worth doing? To put it more starkly, should we simply write off the vast body of work on corporate performance that relies on cross-section correlations? This is probably going too far. Cross-section correlations do contain useful information as long as the investigator is fully aware of all the difficulties of interpretation. In particular, for example, many relevant unobserved factors vary less within industries than across industries. This is just another way of saying that comparing Sainsbury with Tesco may be more rewarding than comparing Sainsbury with Glaxo. In practice, therefore, cross-section analysis of companies should always control for industry (by including industry dummies). Even then, however, interpreting the results always requires particular care.

### Performance from whose point of view?

Aside from a brief discussion of monopoly profits in section 1, we have assumed that the performance of companies is best measured by looking at the rewards accruing to shareholders. However, as we have already noted, if a company manages to achieve a position of significant market power, shareholders, and probably managers and workers as well, will benefit. The company may generate lots of added value but this will often be at the expense of the rest of us. The monopoly rents accruing to the company will be extracted from society as a whole and distributed to shareholders, managers and workers, not only in the form of money but also in the form of on-the-job leisure and so on. This could reduce efficiency, slow down productivity growth and generally have a detrimental impact on national wealth.

Since our ultimate concern is the wealth of nations, this suggests that we may want to measure company performance not only in terms of added value but also in terms of real (total factor) productivity. This eliminates the problem of monopoly rents and allows us to use a measure of performance which is directly related to economic growth. Again, cross-section analysis causes tricky problems but the use of time-series changes can yield accurate estimates of the impact on performance of external factors or internal strategy.

### The business portfolio problem

One final difficulty in measuring corporate performance arises from the fact that many companies consist of a large portfolio of almost separate businesses. Furthermore, it is perfectly possible for each individual business to generate lots of added value or to have high productivity, and yet for the firm operating this portfolio to be bankrupt. This may happen, for example, if the managers of the company had previously paid 'too much' for some of the businesses using borrowed money. Then the market value of the possibly highly successful businesses may be exceeded by the total debt of the company. In practice, this may not be a serious problem because the company can go bankrupt but the businesses can carry on being successful under new ownership. This simply suggests that we must take care when making use of stockmarket valuations to capture aspects of corporate success.

## 4 INVESTIGATING CORPORATE PERFORMANCE

Academics from many disciplines are interested in company performance. Some, notably economists, have often used the black box model of the company. So, if they wish to investigate the impact of exogenous forces on the firm, they assert that the firm uses inputs to produce outputs and chooses the various quantities in order to maximize some objective subject to some exogenous constraints. What goes on inside the firm is not considered: hence 'black box'. While this strategy remains commonplace, some economists have become interested in what goes on in firms. The main argument for remaining aloof is that if firms behave so as to maximize returns to their owners, then we need not really bother ourselves about how they do it. We can predict how they will behave under various circumstances and we can be more or less sure that they will be making efficient use of resources. But suppose we have good reasons for believing that firms are not maximizing in the appropriate way. Then, given that economics is in business to study the allocation of scarce resources, we should want to know what is going on.

What evidence is there that firms are not 'doing their best'? We shall not go into detail at this stage. However, consider the following quote from Michael Porter (1987): 'The corporate strategies of *most* companies have dissipated instead of created shareholder value.' This was in reference to the diversification strategies of 33 of the largest and most prestigious US corporations. If the behaviour of managers in the most successful decentralized economy of the twentieth century is such as to lead to the systematic misallocation of resources, economists cannot but be concerned with their behaviour.

In the remainder of this book, we shall go into this issue in some depth. The overall framework for the analysis is to look at how the external environment of companies influences company performance either directly or, preferably, via its impact on management strategies. The word preferably is used here because, if we can show how a particular exogenous external factor influences management strategies in a particular fashion which then affect firm performance in a given way, we have a more complete understanding of what is going on than if we simply demonstrate that company performance is influenced *either* by a particular external factor *or* by a particular management strategy. It is worth noting at the outset that we are, in many cases, not going to be very successful in this task. However, simply pointing out the gaps in our knowledge will be of some value.

Before we go into details, it is worth noting that our direction of causality (i.e. external factors influence management strategy which, in its turn, influences company performance) is somewhat problematic because management strategies can include attempts to change the external environment, for example, by lobbying government for protectionist measures. Leaving this difficulty aside, we shall focus on three main groups of external factors:

- the structure of ownership, corporate governance and the financial environment;
- the product market environment and the degree of competition;
- the labour market environment, notably the power of unions and labour market legislation.

The areas of management strategy we mainly consider are:

- the organization of the company and its diversification strategy;
- the investment strategy (in the broadest sense, e.g. including R and D and so on);
- the human resource strategy and the organization of production.

The remainder of the book will be devoted to these issues.

## 5 SUMMARY

1 Using super-normal profit or added value (suitably normalized) is a good way of measuring corporate performance as long as (a) all relevant capital is properly measured and (b) we can subtract out monopoly rents.
2 Capital associated with employees' human capital, reputation, advertising and even R and D is very difficult to measure accurately, which suggests that longitudinal analyses of company performance are likely to be more reliable than cross-section analyses.
3 The problem of how to measure monopoly profits can be partly overcome by focusing on productivity as well as super-normal profit.
4 The remainder of the book will be concerned with the impact on corporate performance of (a) the structure of ownership, (b) the extent of competition in the product market and (c) the labour market environment.

### APPENDIX

Given that

$$PV\Pi_t = \int_t^\infty e^{-r(\tau-t)}[R(\tau) - w(\tau)N(\tau) - c(\tau)K(\tau) - p_m(\tau)M(\tau)]d\tau$$

and

$$PVE_t = \int_t^\infty e^{-r(\tau-t)}[R(\tau) - w(\tau)N(\tau) - q(\tau)I(\tau) - p_m(\tau)M(\tau)]d\tau$$

then

$$PVE_t - PV\Pi_t = \int_t^\infty e^{-r(\tau-t)}[c(\tau)K(\tau) - q(\tau)I(\tau)]d\tau. \quad (A1)$$

The standard definition of the cost of capital is $c(\tau) = q(\tau) [r + \delta - \dot{q}/q]$ where $\delta$ is the exponential rate of decay, so that $\dot{K}(\tau) = I(\tau) - \delta K(\tau)$. So

$$\int_t^\infty e^{-r(\tau-t)}q(\tau)I(\tau)d(\tau) = \int_t^\infty e^{-r(\tau-t)}[q(\tau)\dot{K}(\tau) + \delta q(\tau)K(\tau)]d\tau.$$

$$= -q_tK_t + \int_t^\infty e^{-r(\tau-t)}[rq(\tau)K(\tau)$$

$$+ \dot{q}K(\tau) + \delta q(\tau)K(\tau)]d\tau$$

$$= -q_tK_t + \int_t^\infty e^{-r(\tau-t)}c(\tau)K(\tau)d\tau$$

integrating by parts. Substituting this into (A1) yields

$$PVE_t - PV\Pi_t = q_tK_t$$

which is equation (5) in the main text.

## NOTES

1  Investment clearly depends on the marginal returns which correspond to marginal $Q$. The conditions under which average and marginal $Q$ are the same are set out in Hayashi (1982). These are, essentially, constant returns to scale and perfect competition.

2  Is this just a normalization problem? For example, suppose we normalize on value added, using the ratio $((R_t - w_tN_t - c_tK_t)/(w_tN_t + c_tK_t)$, where we ignore inputs other than $N$ and $K$. If there are diminishing returns to scale, it is easy to show that the owners of the firm would like to expand

both $N$ and $K$ beyond the point where this ratio is at its maximum, thereby reducing it.

3 This era of dominance appears to have drawn to a close. At the time of writing, Liverpool were in the bottom half of the Premier Division, though this position improved.

4 The investment expenditures will always appear on the balance sheet under headings such as labour costs. So if we take a period long enough to include these expenditures then there is no trouble.

## REFERENCES

Hayashi, F. (1982) Tobin's marginal $q$ and average $q$: a neo-classical interpretation. *Econometrica*, 50, 214–24.

Kay, J. (1993) *Foundations of Corporate Success*. Oxford: Oxford University Press.

Porter, M. (1987) From competitive advantage to corporate strategy. *Harvard Business Review*, May–June, 43–59.

Prais, S. J. and Wagner, K. (1988) Productivity and management: the training of foremen in Britain and Germany. *National Institute Economic Review*, 123, February.

Steedman, H. and Wagner, K. (1987) A second look at productivity, machinery and skills in Britain and Germany. *National Institute Economic Review*, 122, November.

Stewart, M. (1990) Union wage differentials, product market influences and the division of rents. *Economic Journal*, 100, 1122–37.

# 2

# Ownership, Governance and Corporate Performance I

## INTRODUCTION

The ultimate owners of a firm are its shareholders. For reasonably sized companies, it is most unusual for the majority shareholders actually to manage the business. So there is a fundamental question: are the aims and objectives of the managers aligned with those of the owners of the company? Related to this question is another. How does the financial environment and the system of corporate governance influence the degree to which the interests of managers and owners are aligned? This is the question for this and the next chapter. In order to focus on specific issues, we first describe two stylized forms of financial environment and corporate governance.

*Type I.* Equity markets are large, with the vast majority of the equity in each company under the control of shareholders (either institutions or private investors) who are not closely involved with the firm. In such equity markets, mergers and acquisitions are relatively easy, even hostile ones. It is these latter which exemplify the 'market for corporate control' that exercises external discipline on managers.

*Corporate control/governance associated with type I*
- External control over managers is exerted by the threat of takeover and replacement if they engage in non-present value maximizing behaviour.
- Non-executive or independent directors sit on the board and exercise their judgement in the interests of the shareholders.

*Type II.* Equity markets are organized so that substantial portions of equity in each company are under the control of shareholders who have some degree of long-term commitment to the firm. Hostile takeovers are, as a consequence, more or less impossible.

*Corporate control/governance associated with type II*
- Long-term shareholders or stakeholders exert authority over managers. This authority arises from possession of, or control over, large shareholdings.
- These long-term shareholders or stakeholders nominate directors who can exercise authority when necessary.

Roughly speaking, the type I system corresponds to that operating in the UK and the USA, type II to that in Japan and Germany. Three important arguments have been put forward exemplifying the problems with the type I system.

*Argument 1*   *Short-termism*: the type I system encourages managers to favour short-run objectives at the expense of long-run ones.

*Argument 2   Bad acquisitions*: the type I system encourages managers to engage in acquisition behaviour which reduces shareholder value.

*Argument 3   Less pressure on non-present value maximizing behaviour*: the type I system exerts little pressure on managers to pursue efficiency gains and enables them to engage in non-present value maximizing behaviour, more generally.

Each of these reflects a basic misalignment between the aims and objectives of managers and owners, and claims that the type I system tends to generate these problems. There is also an implication that the type II system would overcome these difficulties. In the remainder of this chapter we shall pursue these arguments at some length. Then, in the next chapter we shall shift the emphasis and analyse a variety of possible mechanisms for corporate control, assessing their effectiveness and how they relate to the type I and type II systems.

# 1   SHORT-TERMISM

Short-termism refers to the notion that 'too much emphasis is placed on short-term profit, which is detrimental to R and D and investment, and hence to long-term growth'. There has been, and still is, a wide-ranging popular debate on this subject, with two types of evidence to the fore. First, it is noted that German and Japanese shareholders appear to have a long-term commitment to the companies in which they own shares, whereas this is not the case in the USA and the UK. It is also noted that industry-financed R and D is around 50 per cent higher in Germany and Japan than in the USA and the UK, with investment rates and growth rates bearing a similar relationship. The conclusion is then drawn that the former causes the latter.

The second type of evidence relies on the experience of both participants in and observers of the market and industrial scene. For example, many US and UK managers are passionately convinced that they are under severe pressure from the stockmarket to behave in a short-term fashion. They convinced Nigel Lawson of this, when he was UK Chancellor. So, in 1986, he remarked, 'The big institutional investors nowadays increasingly react to short-term pressure on investment performance. . .they are unwilling to countenance long-term investment or a sufficient expenditure on R and D.' However, as the famous corporate raider, T. Boone Pickens, noted from the other side, 'Increasing acceptance of the short-term theory. . .has freed executives to scorn any shareholders they choose to identify as short-termers.'

While these arguments put forward in the popular debate may be indicative, they are hardly decisive. Is it possible, first, to construct a satisfactory theoretical foundation for short-termism? Let us distinguish between two different types of behaviour, that is stockmarket myopia and managerial myopia. Both may lead to a short-termist outcome but they have different foundations.

## Stockmarket myopia

The simple argument, hinted at in the quotation from Nigel Lawson, goes as follows. Investors, particularly institutional investors, take a short-term view because fund managers are assessed every quarter on the short-term performance of their portfolios. Therefore they discount the long term 'too heavily' and hence firms which take a long-term view will trade at a discount. It is important to recognize that this implies stockmarket inefficiency. A 'sensible' investor will simply purchase shares in firms which generate long-term returns and she will generate excess profits because such returns will be underpriced in the market.

There is, however, a prior problem. Why should fund-managers take a short-term view just because they are assessed every quarter? In a well functioning equity market, firms which take on long-term investments will be properly valued and the expected performance on these investments will be correctly incorporated into the share price. It is not clear why fund-managers would avoid such shares just because they are assessed frequently. However, things are not quite as straightforward as this.

First, evidence suggests that fund-managers engage in 'excessive' churning of their portfolios and they to do so because of a variety of agency problems associated with the allocation of funds to be managed, and the selection and monitoring of managers. Thus, evidence suggests that the Stock Market Index typically outperforms the majority of actively managed portfolios (see Lakonishok et al., 1992; *Independent on Sunday*, 1993 for clear-cut evidence). Second, fund-managers engage in certain non-optimal strategies as a consequence of frequent performance evaluation. These include: (a) window dressing, i.e. selling poorly performing stocks before evaluation in case these are taken by sponsors as evidence of low ability; and (b) lock-in, where, if the manager finds herself ahead of the Index during a particular quarter, then she 'locks in' the gains by adjusting the portfolio to the Index (see Lakonishok et al., 1991, for evidence on this).

So, for a variety of reasons, some associated with frequent performance deadlines, managers appear to pursue distorted investment strategies which involve selling equity regardless of future expected performance, while attaching a lot of weight to current performance. This may generate stockmarket myopia although, as we have already noted, since other market participants could make a profit by putting their money in firms which make long-term investments, it is not clear that we should expect this outcome.

## Managerial myopia

One obvious reason why managers might behave myopically is that, if they are judged and promoted on current profit performance, they will have an incentive to cut discretionary expenditure (e.g. R and D) if they are likely to be promoted elsewhere before the consequences emerge (see Holmstrom and Ricart i Costa, 1986, for a related model). Of course, firms that organize their managerial incentives in this fashion will be penalized by an all-seeing stockmarket, so this may tend to reduce such behaviour. However, there are circumstances in which managerial myopia will emerge even in the presence of an efficient stockmarket as long as (a) there is asymmetric information (i.e. managers know more than shareholders) and (b) managers are concerned about the current share price (see Stein, 1989).[1]

Thus, in Stein's model there is an optimal earnings stream $(e_t^*)$ which takes the form

$$e_t^* = z_t + v_t, \; z_t = z_{t-1} + u_t, \; v_t \sim N(0, \sigma_v^2), \; u_t \sim N(0, \sigma_u^2) \quad (1)$$

The idea here is that $z_t$ reflects the 'permanent' part of earnings, $v_t$ the 'transitory' part. Suppose that the stockmarket discount rate is $r$ and that managers can generate alternative, sub-optimal, earnings paths by 'borrowing' against future earnings to boost current earnings at an internal rate greater than $r$. Thus if they 'borrow' $b_t$ in period $t$, actual earnings $e_t$ are

$$e_t = e_t^* + b_t - c(b_{t-1}) \quad (2)$$

where $c(b_{t-1})$ reflects the amount they must pay back to cover the borrowing in the previous period. In order to ensure that the borrowing is sub-optimal, we have $c'(0) = (1 + r)$, $c'' > 0$, which implies $c'(b) > (1 + r)$ for all $b > 0$.

The key information asymmetry Stein introduces is that shareholders do not observe $b_t$ or $e_t^*$ but only $e_t^2$. The share price, $P_t$, is given by

$$P_t = \sum_{j=1}^{\infty} E_t(e_{t+j}|I_t)/(1+r)^j \tag{3}$$

where the information set, $I_t$, includes current and past values of earnings.

In steady state equilibrium, suppose that managers undertake a (constant) rate of 'borrowing', $\bar{b}$, in order to boost current earnings. Shareholders, recognizing this motive, will be able to anticipate correctly this borrowing (in steady state equilibrium) and will thus be able to reconstruct an estimate of optimal earnings from (1), namely

$$\hat{e}_t^* = e_t + c(\bar{b}) - \bar{b} \tag{4}$$

Given that they know the form of the earnings process (1), shareholders can use this to forecast future optimal earnings using the forecasting formula

$$E_t(e_{t+k}^*) = \sum_{j=0}^{\infty} \alpha_j \hat{e}_{t-j}^*, \text{ all } k > 0. \tag{5}$$

Note that, because of the form of the earnings process, $E_t(e_{t+k}^*) = E_t(e_{t+1}^*)$, all $k$. The optimal $\alpha_j$ coefficients sum to unity and depend on $\lambda = \sigma_u^2/\sigma_v^2$. In particular, $\alpha_0 = (\lambda+\lambda^2/4)^{\frac{1}{2}} - \lambda/2$, following Muth (1960).

Now consider the situation of the managers. Their role each period is to select $b_t$. In the steady state equilibrium, they know that the shareholders will expect them to choose $\bar{b}$. And, of course, in this equilibrium it will be optimal for them to choose $\bar{b}$. Suppose the managers' objective is a weighted sum of the current share price, $P_t$, and the present value of earnings. Thus the relevant part of the managers' utility is given by[3]

$$U_t = \pi P_t + (1 - \pi)(e_t + e_{t+1}/(1 + r)) \tag{6}$$

We omit future earnings beyond $t + 1$ because these are unaffected by current decisions. So the managers choose $b_t$ to maximize $U_t$. First consider $\partial P_t / \partial b_t$. From (3) and (5), we find that

$$P_t = \frac{1}{r} \sum_{j=0}^{\infty} \alpha_j e_{t-j}$$

and hence, from (2), $\partial P_t / \partial b_t = \alpha_0 / r$. Then, from (2), we also find $\partial e_t / \partial b_t = 1$, $\partial e_{t+1} / \partial b_t = - c'(b_t)$. So the managers will choose $b_t$ to satisfy

$$\partial U_t / \partial b_t = \pi \alpha_0 / r + (1 - \pi)(1 - c'(b_t)/(1 + r)) = 0$$

But, in equilibrium, they choose $b_t = \bar{b}$ and hence $\bar{b}$ satisfies

$$c'(\bar{b}) = (1 + r)\left[ 1 + \frac{\pi \alpha_0}{(1 - \pi)r} \right] \qquad (7)$$

So we can see that the discount rate applied by managers, $c'(\bar{b})$, is, in equilibrium, too high (i.e. greater than the stock-market rate, $1 + r$) as long as the managers put some weight on the current share price in their objective (i.e. $\pi > 0$). The greater this weight, the higher the discount rate used by managers.

It is worth asking why it is that $c'(\bar{b}) = 1 + r$ (i.e. $\bar{b} = 0$) is not an equilibrium. Basically, if the stockmarket does not expect the managers to 'borrow' against future earnings, then they will have every incentive to do so, because this will boost *current* earnings, and hence the share price, via the stockmarket's optimal forecasting mechanism. Furthermore, the share price will rise by more than the fall in present value earnings because the stockmarket does not know that the managers have deliberately reduced future earnings in order to boost current levels.

So we see that the Stein model implies (a) that the discount rate applied by managers is too high (i.e. higher than the rate at which the market discounts future earnings in the same risk class) and (b) that this myopia is more pronounced, the greater the weight placed on the share price in the manager's objectives.

How relevant is the Stein model? There are two key assumptions: asymmetric information and managerial concern about the current share price. The first is uncontroversial. The fact that managers know more about the current and future prospects of the company than the shareholders more or less goes without saying. If it were not the case, few of the problems discussed in this chapter would ever arise. What about the second assumption, that managers are concerned about the current share price? There is no question that, *ceteris paribus*, a higher current share price reduces the threat of takeover, for obvious reasons. So it is no surprise that when US and Japanese executives are asked to rank nine important objectives (factors like product portfolio or market share), the US executives put share price as the second most important objective whereas the Japanese place it last (see Abegglen and Stalk, 1985). Takeovers are not a problem for the Japanese executive.

So the Stein model of managerial myopia does not appear far-fetched. And it does have another very significant implication when it comes to detecting the presence of short-termism. Because managers use a higher discount rate than the market, any announcement of new R and D or capital expenditures should cause the share price to rise. This is because new investments by the company must clear a higher discount rate hurdle than that imposed by the market. Hence any new investment to be undertaken will raise the present value of earnings computed at the market discount rate.

### Evidence on short-termism

(1) We have already noted the 'broad brush' evidence based on comparisons of Japan/Germany with the USA/

UK. In the former, major shareholders hold shares for long periods, have seats on the supervisory board and use 'voice' when things are not going right. In the latter, major shareholders are not, typically, closely involved, tend to 'exit' when things are going badly and have no long-term commitment. The myopia arises (via the results of the Stein model) because managers are more concerned with the current share price *and* there is greater informational asymmetry in the latter system.

The importance of this last is confirmed by the results of Cable (1985) and Hoshi et al. (1991). Cable demonstrates that bank involvement in German companies leads to superior financial performance via what he terms 'the internal capital markets hypothesis'. This hypothesis effectively says that close involvement of a bank improves the investment performance of a company by removing the informational asymmetries between investor and lender. Hoshi et al. provide direct evidence of this in the Japanese context. They discover that investment in those firms which do *not* have a long-term relationship with their banks is responsive to internally generated cash flow. This is not the case for those with long-term banking relationships. The argument here is that the responsiveness of investment to cash flow is a symptom of asymmetric information. If managers wish to invest more than the funds they themselves control, they have to go outside to the market and pay a premium because of the ignorance of the market concerning the firm's prospects. This problem does not arise when the institutions providing the funds have a long-term relationship with the company.

(2)   There is a great deal of evidence that R and D or capital expenditure announcements tend to raise stock prices (see, for example, McConnell and Muscarella, 1985; Office of the Chief Economist, SEC, 1985; other references are cited in Hall, 1991, footnote 20). This is taken by some to

be evidence against short-termism but, as we have already noted, it is evidence in favour of the Stein model and is, therefore, perfectly consistent with managerial myopia.

The evidence also suggests that increased institutional stockholdings are not associated with reductions in R and D, that high R and D does not increase vulnerability to takeover (see, again, Office of the Chief Economist, SEC, 1985) and that firms which are acquired do not have higher R and D expenditures (relative to sales) than firms in the same industry which are not acquired (Hall, 1988). While this is evidence against crude stockmarket myopia theories it is not really relevant to managerial myopia, which assumes stockmarket efficiency.

(3)   Firms under threat of takeover appear to reduce both their investment and their R and D to sales ratios (the latter substantially: see Ashmore, 1990), presumably in an attempt to raise current earnings and the current share price. This is again consistent with the Stein model of managerial myopia. However, an apparently adverse piece of evidence is presented by Meulbroek et al. (1990). They find that firms whose shareholders pass anti-takeover amendments, thereby increasing the protection of their managers against takeover, subsequently *reduce* their R and D expenditures relative to the industry average. So increasing managerial security apparently *reduces* long-term investment expenditure. This may, however, be explained by noting that firms which pass anti-takeover amendments are typically those under threat and would, on the evidence of Ashmore, be simultaneously reducing R and D and investment expenditures. That is, the passing of anti-takeover amendments is part of a package of defensive measures which also includes R and D reduction. There is no causal relationship between the two.

(4)   There is some direct evidence that excessive discounting of expected long-term earnings appears in UK stock

prices (Nickell and Wadhwani, 1987; Miles, 1992). This is based on the following type of model. Ignoring taxes, with no myopia the price of security $j$, $P_j$, satisfies

$$P_{jt} = \sum_{i=1}^{N} \frac{E[D_{jt+i}]}{[1 + r_{t\,t+i} + \pi_j]^i} + \frac{E[P_{j\,t+N}]}{[1 + r_{t\,t+N} + \pi_j]^N} \qquad (8)$$

where $r_{t\,t+i}$ is the annual 'safe' discount rate from $t$ to $t + i$, $\pi_j$ is the risk premium associated with security $j$, $D_{j\,t+i}$ is the dividend payment at $t + i$ and E is the expectation operator.

To make this operational, Miles proxies the risk premium by a linear function of the beta for security $j$, $\beta_j$, and the debt gearing of the company, $z_j$. Thus we have

$$\pi_j = a_1\beta_j + a_2 z_j \qquad (9)$$

where $a_1$ would reflect the difference between the expected return on the market portfolio and the safe rate (under the assumptions of the Capital Asset Pricing Model) and $a_2$ would be positive if future interest rates were uncertain. So, in order to test for stockmarket myopia, Miles estimates a series of equations of the form

$$P_{jt} = \sum_{i=1}^{N} \frac{x^i E[D_{jt+i}]}{[1 + r_{t\,t+i} + a_1\beta_j + a_2 z_j]^i} + \frac{E[P_{j\,t+N}]}{[1 + r_{t\,t+N} + a_1\beta_j + a_2 z_j]^N}$$

and finds $x$ to be 0.925 (significantly different from unity). Of course, the major difficulties with obtaining convincing evidence are modelling the risk premium[4] and finding valid instruments to deal with the expectational regressors. Miles may not have solved these problems to everyone's satisfaction but if we take his results at face value, they indicate that projects with a five-year horizon need to be around 40 per cent more profitable than would be optimal, in order to satisfy the market. This of course implies serious stock-market inefficiency. These numbers are consistent with the fact, noted in Marsh (1991), that UK companies continue, in the main, to use crude pay-back methods for investment appraisal. This generates a bias towards quick-return projects and against investment proposals with high returns which accrue only after a considerable period.

(5)   Finally, there is evidence presented by Brickley et al. (1985) and Tehranian and Waegelein (1985) on the stock price effects of announcements of new managerial compensation schemes. The introduction of long-range (over one year) compensation schemes for managers generates an average stock price rise of 2 per cent whereas the introduction of short-range compensation schemes generates an 11 per cent rise in stock prices and an 8 per cent abnormal return over the subsequent 11 months. This would appear to suggest that short-term compensation controls the stock price and generates a strong incentive for managers to engage in searching out short-term profit opportunities. However, as Board et al. (1990) note, these results could simply reflect opportunistic behaviour on the part of managers who know that good results are in the offing and set up a compensation scheme to take advantage of this. When this is announced, their inside information is effectively transmitted to shareholders and the share price goes up.

So the evidence is mixed. However, there is very little evidence which conflicts with the existence of some degree of managerial myopia, particularly in circumstances where managers are confronted with pressure from the capital market which leads them to place the current share price and current earnings high on their list of objectives. Furthermore, this pressure appears to arise particularly in circumstances where there are large institutional shareholders whose fund-managers are judged on short-term results and use 'exit' rather than 'voice' to express dissatisfaction. Thus, we can conclude that there is some evidence to suggest that the UK/USA type I system described in the introduction generates more short-termism, via the managerial myopia mechanism, than the Germany / Japan type II system. However, there is no evidence on the extent or cost of this short-termism. Indeed, it might be argued that the type II system generates excessive long-termism, allowing companies to persist with loss-making business for far too long. For example, the German company Siemens has made enormous losses in semiconductors and computers over a very long period. So the overall importance of short-termism remains an open question.

## 2  BAD ACQUISITIONS

As we have already noted in the introduction to this chapter, in type I financial environments such as the USA and UK, the behaviour of large institutional investors implies that acquisitions, even if they are hostile, are comparatively straightforward. In type II environments, such as in Germany and Japan, hostile acquisitions are more or less impossible although friendly ones are not uncommon. The question that concerns us here is whether acquisitions, especially hostile ones, are beneficial to the acquiring firms. In particular, does the type I financial environment and system of corporate governance allow the managers of acquiring firms to make acquisitions which are detrimental to their shareholders or other stakeholders? Porter (1987), for example, is quite clear-cut on this question, arguing that the acquisition strategy pursued by many large US corporations is against the interests of shareholders.

Some of the facts about acquisitions are uncontroversial. In the short run, the shareholders of acquiring firms benefit slightly, if at all, whereas those of acquired firms typically benefit a lot. Thus, using data on 1900 mergers in the UK, Franks and Harris (1989) find that in the six-month period starting four months prior to the bid, the shareholders of the acquiring firm achieve a 7 per cent gain whereas the shareholders of the target firm gain to the tune of 30 per cent. Results reported in Hughes (1989) and Peacock and Bannock (1991) are broadly consistent with this story. In the United States, Bradley et al. (1988) find that, in the 1980s, shareholders in the acquiring firms suffered a small loss (just under 3 per cent) whereas those in the target firms gained around 35 per cent. Similar results are reported in Asquith et al. (1990) and Caves (1989), although somewhat less biased in favour of the target.

Where do these large rents which accrue to the shareholders actually come from? The obvious sources are efficiency gains and wealth transfers from other stakeholders, notably labour (Shleifer and Summers, 1988). Considering the latter first, the most clear-cut evidence is provided by Lichtenberg and Siegel (1990a; 1992), who find that following an ownership change, there is a substantial reduction in overhead labour relative to production labour (around 11 per cent) and also a reduction in the relative wages of the former (around 4 per cent). This is consistent with more anecdotal evidence concerning the behaviour of corporate raiders. As Henry Kravis (1989) remarks, 'People who produce things will stay. We look at the people who report to people who report to people.'[5] Thus, for example, after Hansen had acquired the London Brick Company, the number of head office staff was cut dramatically (by more than 90 per cent).

In contrast, there is more or less no evidence that direct wage concessions contribute significantly to takeover premia (see Rossett, 1990) or that union-busting or union dilution are the consequences of mergers (Fallick and Hassett, 1990). The evidence regarding efficiency gains is very mixed. First, Ravenscraft and Scherer (1987), using US line-of-business data, conclude that lines of business acquired during the 1960s and early 1970s were highly profitable before mergers, but that profitability subsequently declined. However, Lichtenberg and Siegel (1987) find that manufacturing *plants* in the USA which had ownership changes in the period 1974–7 experienced a 0.8 percentage point increase in annual total factor productivity growth relative to those which had no ownership change. They also found that, prior to the change in ownership, these same plants had significantly lower total factor productivity than the average plant in the same industry. Thus, the evidence suggests that poorly performing plants tended to change owners and that subsequently they started to 'catch up' towards the average. Healy et al. (1990) also find that, for the 50 biggest US takeovers in the period 1979–83, operating cash flow performance relative to the industry improved in the five years subsequent to the takeover.

Lichtenberg and Siegel suggest that these results may be explained by looking at the different time periods involved. The Ravenscraft and Scherer sample contains many of the large conglomerates which were formed in the 1960s and subsequently divested themselves of the majority of their acquisitions, particularly those which were in businesses unrelated to their core activities (see Porter, 1987, for example). These divestitures were as a result of declining profitability and it is, presumably, many of these which find their way into the sample of plants used by Lichtenberg and Siegel. The Lichtenberg and Siegel results then indicate that these plants started doing better under their new owners. These results are consistent with the view that the building of conglomerates in the 1960s in the United States was detrimental to performance, and the subsequent break-up of these conglomerates, with the pieces typically being absorbed by companies in related businesses, represented a significant improvement (see Bhagat et al., 1990, for example). Indeed, the view that companies should 'stick to their knitting'[6] became almost universally accepted following the publication of the extraordinarily influential book *In Search of Excellence* by Peters and Waterman in 1982. Here, they identify the key characteristics of 'excellent companies', and the ability to concentrate on what they do best is one of these. This is an issue to which we shall return later.

Evidence on the performance of acquired companies in the UK is more generally negative. Hughes (1989) surveys the evidence and concludes that, on average, there have not been efficiency gains following mergers. This contradicts the evidence presented for the USA by Lichtenberg and Siegel, and Lichtenberg (1992, chapter 6) contains a pointer to the reason for this. Using data on mergers and acquisitions for some 22 countries during the period 1988–90, he finds that while acquired firms performed notably badly prior to acquisition in the United States, this pattern did not appear in firms outside the United States. So while in the USA there was 'room for improvement' in the sense that the acquired firms were significantly below average performers in the years prior to acquisition, outside the USA acquired firms were about average. Why this should be so remains unclear.

## Why acquisitions?

Having seen the consequences of acquisitions, we next investigate why firms wish to diversify by the acquisition route. So let us list some of the reasons for this behaviour along with the potential gains to the shareholders and managers of the acquiring firm. It is important to recognize that the reasons given in this list are *not* mutually exclusive and that any or all of them may be at work.

1   *Synergies.* In related diversification, there are opportunities for allocating and transferring technical and managerial skills of the right type. These would exploit interrelationships between divisions in marketing, R and D, production and purchasing. They can also, of course, lead to increases in market power. When firms diversify into unrelated areas, they must rely on utilizing

financial and managerial competencies which may be particularly valuable if the target is grossly inefficient. Shareholder gains are significant if efficiency can be improved. Managerial gains are minimal.

2   *Volatility reduction.* Diversification may lead to a reduction in the volatility of earnings and profits in the merged company. This is particularly true in the case of unrelated diversification into areas where market fluctuations are not highly correlated with those of the acquiring firm. Shareholder gains are minimal since shareholders can diversify anyway via the stockmarket. Managerial gains may be significant because the security of managers is increased. For example, a reduction in volatility may reduce the risk of bankruptcy and resulting managerial job-loss.

3   *Managerial advancement.* Promotion possibilities for managers may well improve in a larger unit, so they can improve their lot without having to move to another employer. Shareholder gains could exist if firms are enabled to retain their best managers. Note that it is the best who are most likely to quit. Managerial gains are obvious.

4   *Managerial power.* Managers may wish to engage in mergers and acquisitions simply because they gain in power and status by managing a larger volume of assets. Shareholder gains are zero or negative. Managerial gains are obvious.

5   *Managerial hubris.* The notion here (Roll, 1986) is simply that managers of successful firms become overconfident and think they can manage anything. Shareholder gains are zero or negative. Managerial gains are obvious.

It is clear from this list that while shareholders may gain from mergers and acquisitions as long as they are driven by synergies of various kinds leading to improvements in efficiency, managers may gain from acquisitions in situations where shareholders receive no direct benefit or indeed may even lose out. Given information asymmetries, there is clearly a danger that such acquisitions may occur. So what is the evidence that managers pursue objectives in their acquisitions strategy which are not to the advantage of shareholders?

Let us begin with some general pieces of evidence. Typically, low management ownership in the bidding firm is associated with lower returns from making acquisitions (Lewellen et al., 1985; You et al., 1986). This suggests that managers with low financial incentives to maximize market value tend to pursue a poorer acquisition strategy, and, presumably, shareholders are unable to prevent this.

Turning to the issue of related versus unrelated acquisitions, in the 1980s the latter tended to reduce bidder returns (Morck et al., 1990; Singh and Montgomery, 1987).[7] Furthermore, Hill and Snell (1988) find that, in a sample of 94 large firms in research-intensive industries, the weaker are shareholders, the more likely is the firm to make unrelated acquisitions. They also find that this tendency is not muted by having outsiders on the board, an issue to which we shall return in due course. So again we find that when managers are free to do so, they tend to make poorer acquisitions.

Concerning the specific motives listed above, Amihud and Lev (1981) present some evidence that manager-controlled firms are more likely to engage in volatility-reducing diversification than owner-controlled firms (motive 2).[8] The results of Morck et al. (1990) indicate that buying growth reduces bidders' returns, and thus bidders tend to 'overpay' for fast-growing companies. This suggests that managers like growth for its own sake, which is consistent with the managerial advancement and managerial power motives (3 and 4). Finally, it seems to be the case that better managers make better acquisitions (Lang et al., 1989; Morck et al., 1990), which is not really consistent with the hubris explanation of Roll (1986) (motive 5).

Overall, therefore, there is some evidence that managers are able to pursue acquisition strategies which are not in the best interests of shareholders in situations where, because of the agency problems arising from asymmetric information, they are free to do so. All this evidence comes from the type I system in which acquisitions, particularly hostile ones, are relatively straightforward. There is little systematic evidence from type II systems. However, casual empiricism suggests that managers under the type II system are quite able to make bad acquisitions. Indeed, with their close relationships with banks, friendly acquisitions are relatively straightforward.

A classic example is provided by the German manufacturer of Mercedes cars, Daimler-Benz, which since the mid-1980s has diversified extensively via acquisition into a wide range of unrelated activities, from aerospace and electronics to financial services and software. With its share price virtually halving since its 1986 peak, it is generally agreed that this acquisition strategy has not been to the benefit of shareholders (see *The Economist*, 26 June 1993, and *Manager Magazin*, September 1993, for full details). Overall, therefore, while we know that the type I system allows bad acquisitions, there is no strong evidence that the type II system does not.

## 3  NON-PRESENT VALUE MAXIMIZING BEHAVIOUR

In the previous two sections, we have focused on two alleged consequences of type I environments, namely short-termism and bad acquisition strategy. Here, we look at the extent to which the type I environment might allow non-present value maximizing behaviour more generally. A useful perspective on this question is provided by the 'free cash flow' theory of Jensen (see Jensen, 1988, pp. 28–9, for a full discussion). Free cash flow is the flow of corporate earnings in excess of that required to fund all of a firm's projects that have positive net present value. In order to maximize the benefit to shareholders, such free cash flow should be paid out in the form of dividends.

Jensen argues that because of the weakness of shareholder control over managers, free cash flow is often wasted. Much of this waste takes the form of poor unrelated acquisitions, which we have already discussed, but some involves bad investment decisions more generally. In Jensen (1988), he cites the example of the US oil industry in the first half of the 1980s. Because of the high price of oil following the second oil shock in 1979, oil companies had enormous cash flows. These excess resources were not, however, distributed to shareholders, but were spent on extensive exploration and development activity even though the returns were below the cost of capital.

The free cash flow theory also suggests that the existence of debt may provide an incentive for managers to operate at a higher level of efficiency. As Jensen (1988, p. 29) notes, 'Debt reduces the agency cost of free cash flow by reducing the cash flow available for spending at the discretion of managers.' The idea is that managers *must* pay out the interest on the debt whereas they have discretion on the size of dividend payments. If they fail in the former, the firm goes bankrupt, an outcome which managers have every incentive to avoid. So debt exercises a disciplinary role, leading to improved efficiency.

Evidence on this question is provided in an analysis of productivity changes consequent on leveraged buyouts (LBOs) by Lichtenberg and Siegel (1990b). They find that total factor productivity improves in plants subject to LBOs relative to plants in the same industry not subject to LBOs. This could, however, also be owing to the increased management stake in the company following an LBO, which increases the incentive of managers to perform well. More direct evidence is presented by Nickell et al. (1992), who find that higher debt burdens are, *ceteris paribus*, associated with both higher total factor productivity and higher total factor productivity growth in their analysis of a panel of UK manufacturing companies.

## SUMMARY AND CONCLUSION

In this chapter we have considered the evidence on some of the consequences of a type I form of financial environment and system of corporate governance. Recall that in a type I system, the majority of the equity in a company is controlled by shareholders who are not closely involved with the firm. Relative to the type II system, where the majority of shareholders have some degree of long-term commitment to the company, mergers and acquisitions, particularly hostile ones, are relatively straightforward and act as an external discipline on managers. The following conclusions have been reached.

1 There is some evidence that the type I system leads to short-termism. The open stockmarket environment allied to asymmetric information leads to managerial myopia – that is, managers have an incentive to favour short-run objectives.

2 The type I system allows managers to pursue an acquisition strategy which reduces shareholder returns, because they have the freedom to act on motives which are not aligned to the objectives of shareholders. However, there is no evidence that managers in the type II system are particularly restricted in their freedom to make bad acquisitions.

3 There is some evidence that the type I system allows managers to engage in non-present value maximizing behaviour generally.

In the light of these results, what can we say more generally about the best form of financial environment and corporate governance? In particular, can we say that the type II model is better? This issue we shall pursue in the next chapter.

## NOTES

1   Miller and Rock (1985) have a related model with similar implications.
2   This supposes that some investment expenditures are 'invisible'. Examples of such expenditures include the provision of specific human capital, expenditure of resources on quality control, cutting prices to boost market share in the presence of switching costs and so on.
3   This is slightly different from the objective in Stein's paper.
4   The problem is that a suitably time varying risk premium, which is not observed, can explain anything.
5   Quoted in Lichtenberg and Siegel (1992).
6   That is, concentrate on their areas of core expertise.
7   Asquith et al. (1990) find the opposite result, perhaps because they use a sample which excludes tender offers.
8   This is consistent with the results of Hill and Snell (1988).

## REFERENCES

Abegglen, J. and Stalk, G. (1985) *Kaisha, the Japanese Corporation*. New York: Basic Books.
Amihud, Y. and Lev, B. (1981) Risk reduction as a managerial motive for conglomerate mergers. *Bell Journal of Economics*, 12, 605–17.
Ashmore, D. (1990) Examining the effects of takeover pressure on research and development intensity. Harvard University Senior Honours Thesis.

Asquith, D., Opler, T. C. and Weston, J. F. (1990) The size and distribution of shareholder wealth gains from mergers: evidence from the takeover boom of the 1980s. UCLA Program in Applied Econometrics D.P. No. 11.

Bhagat, S., Schleifer, A. and Vishny, R. W. (1990) Hostile takeovers in the 1980s: the return to corporate specialization. *Brookings Papers on Economic Activity, Microeconomics Issue*, 1–84.

Board, J., Delargy, R. and Tonks, I. (1990) Short-termism: some conceptual issues. London School of Economics, mimeo.

Bradley, M., Desai, A. and Kim, E. H. (1988) Synergistic gains from corporate acquisitions and their division between stockholders of target and acquiring firms. *Journal of Financial Economics*, 17, 3–40.

Brickley, A. J., Bhagat, S. and Lease, R. C. (1985) The impact of long-range managerial compensation plans on shareholder wealth. *Journal of Accounting and Economics*, 7, 115–29.

Cable, J. (1985) Capital market information and industrial performance: the role of West German banks. *Economic Journal*, 95, 118–32.

Caves, R. E. (1989) Mergers, takeovers and economic efficiency. *International Journal of Industrial Organization*, 7, 151–74.

Fallick, B. C. and Hassett, K. (1990) Unionization and acquisitions. UCLA Program in Applied Econometrics D.P. No. 31.

Franks, J. and Harris, R. (1989) Shareholder wealth effects of UK takeovers: implications for merger policy. In J. Fairburn and J. Kay (eds), *Mergers and Merger Policy*. Oxford: Oxford University Press.

Hall, B. H. (1988) The effect of takeover activity on corporate research and development. In A. J. Auerback (ed.), *Corporate Takeovers: Causes and Consequences*. Chicago: University of Chicago Press.

Hall, B. H. (1991) Corporate restructuring and investment horizons. NBER Working Paper No. 3794, Cambridge MA.

Healy, P., Palepu, K. G. and Ruback, R. S. (1990) Does corporate performance improve after mergers? NBER Working Paper Number 3348, Cambridge, MA.

Hill, C. W. L. and Snell, S. A. (1988) External control, corporate strategy, and firm performance in research intensive industries. *Strategic Management Journal*, 9, 577–90.

Holmstrom, B. and Ricart i Costa, J. (1986) Managerial incentives and capital management. *Quarterly Journal of Economics*, 101, 835–60.

Hoshi, T., Kashyap, A. and Scharfstein, D. (1991) Corporate structure, liquidity and investment: evidence from Japanese industrial groups. *Quarterly Journal of Economics*, 106, 33–60.

Hughes, A. (1989) The impact of merger: a survey of empirical evidence for the UK. In J. Fairburn and J. Kay (eds), *Mergers and Merger Policy*. Oxford: Oxford University Press.

*Independent on Sunday* (1993) Why investors should not put too much trust in the experts. Business section, 15 August, 3–4.

Jensen, M. C. (1988) Takeovers: their causes and consequences. *Journal of Economic Perspectives*, 2, Winter, 21–48.

Kravis, H. (1989) Greed really turns me off. *Fortune*, 2 January, 69–71.

Lakonishok, J., Shleifer, A., Thaler, R. and Vishny, R. (1991) Window dressing by pension fund managers. *American Economic Review, Papers and Proceedings*, 81, 227–31.

Lakonishok, J., Shleifer, A. and Vishny, R. W. (1992) The structure and performance of the money management industry. *Brookings Papers on Economic Activity, Microeconomics*, 339–79.

Lang, L., Stulz, R. M. and Walking, R. A. (1989) Tobin's *q* and the gains from successful tender offers. *Journal of Financial Economics*, 24, 137–54.

Lewellen, W., Roderer, C. and Rosenfield, A. (1985) Merger decisions and executive stock ownership in acquiring firms. *Journal of Accounting and Economics*, 7, 209–31.

Lichtenberg, F. R. (1992) *Corporate Takeovers and Productivity*. Cambridge, MA: MIT Press.

Lichtenberg, F. R. and Siegel, D. (1987) Productivity and changes in ownership of manufacturing plants. *Brookings Papers on Economic Activity, Special Issue on Microeconomics*, 643–73.

Lichtenberg, F. and Siegel, D. (1990a) The effect of ownership changes on the employment and wages of central office and other personnel. *Journal of Law and Economics*, 33, 383–408.

Lichtenberg, F. R. and Siegel, D. (1990b) The effects of leveraged buyouts on productivity and related aspects of firm behaviour. *Journal of Financial Economics*, 25, 165–94.

Lichtenberg, F. and Siegel, D. (1992) Takeovers and corporate overhead. In F. R. Lichtenberg, *Corporate Takeovers and Productivity*. Cambridge, MA: MIT Press.

McConnell, J. J. and Muscarella, C. J. (1985) 'Corporate capital expenditures and the market value of the firm. *Journal of Financial Economics*, 14, 399–422.

Marsh, P. (1991) Market assessment of company performance. NEDO Conference Paper on Capital Markets and Company Success, November.

Meulbroek, L. K., Mitchell, M. L., Mulherin, J. H., Nelter, J. M. and Poulson, A. B. (1990) Shark repellents and managerial myopia. *Journal of Political Economy*, 98, 1108–1117.

Miles, D. (1992) Testing for short termism in the UK stock market. Bank of England, Working Paper No. 4.

Miller, M. and Rock, K. (1985) Dividend policy under asymmetric information. *Journal of Finance*, XL, 1031–51.

Morck, R., Shleifer, A. and Vishny, R. W. (1990) Do managerial objectives drive bad acquisitions? *Journal of Finance*, XLV, 31–48.

Muth, R. (1960) Optimal properties of exponentially weighted forecasts. *Journal of the American Statistical Association*, 55, 299–306.

Nickell, S. J. and Wadhwani, S. (1987) Myopia, the dividend puzzle, and share prices. LSE Centre for Labour Economics, Discussion Paper No. 272.

Nickell, S. J., Wadhwani, S. and Wall, M. (1992) Productivity growth in UK companies, 1975–86. *European Economic Review*, 36, 1055–91.

Offices of the Chief Economist, Securities and Exchange Commission (1985) Institutional ownership, tender offers and long term investment.

Peacock, A. and Bannock, G. (1991) *Corporate Takeovers and the Public Interest*. Edinburgh: David Hume Institute.

Porter, M. (1987) From competitive advantage to corporate strategy. *Harvard Business Review,* May–June, 43–59.

Ravenscraft, D. J. and Scherer, F. M. (1987) *Mergers, Sell-offs and Economic Efficiency.* Washington, DC: Brookings Institution.

Roll, R. (1986) The hubris hypothesis of corporate takeovers. *Journal of Business,* 59, 197–216.

Rossett, J. (1990) Do union wealth concessions explain takeover premiums? The evidence on contract wages. *Journal of Financial Economics,* 27, 263–82.

Shleifer, A. and Summers, L. H. (1988) Breach of trust in hostile takeovers. In A. J. Auerbach (ed.), *Corporate Takeovers: Causes and Consequences.* Chicago: University of Chicago Press.

Singh, H. and Montgomery, C. A. (1987) Corporate acquisition strategies and economic performance. *Strategic Management Journal,* 8, 377–86.

Stein, J. C. (1989) Efficient capital markets, inefficient firms: a model of myopic corporate behaviour. *Quarterly Journal of Economics,* 104, 773–87.

Tehranian, H. and Waegelein, J. F. (1985) Market reaction to short-term executive compensation plan adoption. *Journal of Accounting and Economics,* 7, 131–44.

You, V. L., Caves, R. E., Henry, J. S. and Smith M. M. (1986) Mergers and bidders' wealth: managerial and strategic factors. In L. G. Thomas (ed.), *The Economics of Strategic Planning.* Boston: Lexington Books.

# Ownership, Governance and Corporate Performance II

## INTRODUCTION

In the previous chapter we focused on two distinct types of corporate governance associated with two forms of financial environment. Type I refers to a system where shareholders are not closely involved with the company and external control over managers is exerted by the threat of takeover and replacement if they engage in non-present value maximizing behaviour. Internal control is exerted by non-executive or independent directors who act in the interests of the shareholders. In the type II system, shareholders have some degree of long-term commitment to the company and exercise direct authority over managers.

In Chapter 2, we discussed how the type I system produces situations in which the aims and objectives of managers are not aligned with those of the owners of the company. Our aim here is to look more closely at the mechanisms by which the objectives of managers and owners can be more closely aligned, and whether the type II system is particularly good at providing these mechanisms.

As we have already noted, the basic difficulty is that the managers know what is going on in the company and the owners, typically, do not. In what follows, we consider a number of mechanisms to deal with the consequences of this informational asymmetry. These are, first, the market for corporate control and the takeover mechanism; second, the use of incentive contracts for managers; third, the employment of non-executive or independent directors; fourth, the direct exercise of authority by shareholders, typically via banks.

# 1 HOSTILE TAKEOVERS AND THE MARKET FOR CORPORATE CONTROL

Hostile takeovers are possible in the type I system but effectively impossible in the type II alternative. So they represent a strong distinguishing characteristic. In chapter 2 we have seen how the very ease of acquisition and merger in the type I system enables managers to pursue loss-making acquisition strategies. Is this compensated for by the efficiency-inducing threat of hostile takeover? How does this threat work? If the management of a company is underperforming (engaging in non-present value maximizing behaviour), this will be reflected in a 'low' stockmarket valuation. Another managerial team can then buy the company, sack the existing managers, impose present value maximizing behaviour on the company, raise the stockmarket valuation and pocket the increase. Since the old management will lose heavily from this process, it has every incentive to avoid it by not underperforming in the first place.

Grossman and Hart (1980) point out a serious problem with this argument. Consider a small shareholder in a target company who sees a new management wanting to take it over. Suppose the potential management makes an offer at a price which does not fully reflect the prospective increased profits under new management. Then the small shareholder has no incentive to sell. Why? First, it is important to recognize that, being a small shareholder, her action does not influence the probability of success of the takeover. Suppose the takeover goes ahead. By not selling, her shares in the company will appreciate by an amount which *fully* reflects the increased profits generated by the new management. So she will not sell until the offer price fully reflects these increased profits. Consequently, the takeover will not succeed unless this occurs, and the bidding management makes no gains. So potentially superior managers have no incentive to bid for badly managed companies.

Does this argument stand up in practice? One possible way around the problem is for the bidders to take a stake in the target prior to announcing a bid. The size of this stake is generally subject to legal limits (typically 5 to 10 per cent) but this may, nevertheless, generate a sizeable reward. An alternative is for the bidders to divert gains away from those target shareholders who do not accept. However, despite these possibilities, it remains true that the shareholders of target firms obtain most of the rewards, although this is partly because of competition between bidders (see Asquith et al., 1990). Nevertheless, the numerous takeovers that actually occur indicate that the rewards to bidding *managements* appear to be substantial enough *as long as the total gains are large*, the average total gains being around 30 per cent of the value of the target. Given that this level of total gains appears to be a requirement for a successful takeover, it might be argued that mismanagement which reduces a firm's value by only 15 per cent, say, will go unpunished. Furthermore, low quality managers can protect their positions by instituting various wasteful takeover defence mechanisms. A convenient summary of these may be found in Jarrell et al. (1988), who indicate that the most effective defences tend to reduce the wealth of the target shareholders when they are instituted.

So, in the light of this, does the existence of the threat of a hostile takeover act as a disciplinary device in practice? Generally, the evidence suggests that firms subject to hostile bids do not appear to be performing particularly badly. Thus Franks and Mayer (1992) report that the share price and dividend performance of hostile bid targets in Britain in the mid-1980s was not significantly different from the performance of accepted bid targets. Furthermore, the performance of both was much better than that of firms in the lowest deciles of share performance. Similar results are found by Martin and McConnell (1991). However, the results of Shleifer and Vishny (1988) indicate that the takeover mechanism seems to work particularly well in helping the reorganization of declining industries. Overall, then, the hostile takeover is an expensive and disruptive mechanism and it does not seem very effective as a disciplinary device, except, perhaps, in the most blatant cases of inefficiency.

## 2 INTERNAL CONTROL: INCENTIVE CONTRACTS

In any situation where there are informational asymmetries, we can expect to see incentive contracts of various kinds, and this would apply in both type I and type II economies. The particular problem we are faced with here is that the owners of the firm do not know all the details relevant to an evaluation of the firm's performance. The manager may know but there is no reason why she should tell the owners. In order to give the manager some incentive to work hard, the obvious mechanism is to give her some stake in the business. In order to analyse this intuition, consider the following stylized situation.

The owner of a company is concerned with the profit. This is an increasing function of (a) the manager's effort and (b) random shocks which may be firm specific, industry specific or aggregate. The manager is averse to both risk and effort, and has an alternative option to working in this company. Neither effort nor the shocks can be observed, *ex post*, only the profit. Consider two extreme forms of managerial contract. First is the standard wage contract. The owners pay the manager a fixed wage (which is set to be just preferable to her alternative), and keep the rest of the profit. Second is a fixed dividend contract (or debt contract). The owners pay themselves a fixed dividend and the manager keeps the rest of the profit. Under the first contract, the manager will provide the smallest level of effort which she can get away with. Under the second, she will provide a great deal of effort but she will need compensation for the large amount of risk she has to bear. So the optimal contract will generally be somewhere between these two extremes. The manager's reward will depend on the profit outcome, to some extent.[1]

This simple framework tells us more. The problem for the owner is disentangling the manager's effort from the random shocks. He wants to reward her for the former and ignore the latter. But some shocks are aggregate, that is, they apply to the whole economy and will affect the profits of many firms in the same way. Other shocks are industry specific, that is, they affect all the firms in the industry in a similar fashion. In order to control for shocks of this type, all the owner has to do is to look at the profit outcome of his firm *relative* to that of other firms, either throughout the economy or within the same industry. Rewarding the manager on the basis of these *relative* performance measures will be more effective than just using absolute profit figures because the profits of the firm relative to its industrial competitors are more closely related to the manager's effort (see Nalebuff and Stiglitz, 1983, for example).

Our analysis indicates that we should expect to see managerial remuneration directly related to company performance and, more particularly, to performance relative to that of other companies in the same industry. So does managerial pay have these characteristics, and if so, does this work?

## The evidence on managerial pay

The first question to ask is whether or not managerial pay is actually related to company performance. The evidence here is clear. There is a positive relationship. In the United States, the pay of chief executive officers (CEOs) is around $100–150 per annum higher for every $1 million increase in shareholder returns (see Murphy, 1985, 1986; Coughlin and Schmidt, 1985; Barro and Barro, 1991; and the excellent survey by Rosen, 1990). Effects of the same order of magnitude are reported for the United Kingdom (Main, 1991) and Japan (Kaplan, 1991). The US numbers are all based on regressions using log (compensation) as the dependent variable. Significantly smaller estimates are reported by Jensen and Murphy (1990), who use dollar compensation as the dependent variable rather than its log. In Rosen's view, the log form provides the more reliable estimates,[2] and the preferred numbers indicate that the impact of a serious mistake on the wealth of a CEO is fairly significant. For example, Rosen computes that a decline of around $0.5 billion in the stock value of a company (about 10 per cent for the average company in the relevant sample) would cost the CEO a $50 000 per annum pay cut (again about 10 per cent).

Not only should we expect the pay of managers to be performance related, we should also expect it to be strongly associated with performance relative to other firms, particularly those in the same industry. The evidence on this is mixed. Antle and Smith (1986) and Barro and Barro (1990) find no strong association between managerial compensation and relative performance. However, in a comprehensive analysis, Gibbons and Murphy (1990) find a strong association between CEO pay and relative performance measures, although, somewhat surprisingly, they find some tendency for the most important comparison group to be the rest of the economy rather than just those firms in the same industry. They also show that the data used by Antle and Smith yield quite similar results if the same specification is used.

Related to this are investigations of CEO turnover which indicate that, in the United States, decisions to replace CEOs are based, in part, on recent relative performance, although again performance relative to the aggregate of firms seems more important than that relative to other firms in the same industry (Warner et al., 1988; Gibbons and Murphy, 1990). Evidence for Japan and Germany (Kaplan, 1992, 1993) indicates that, in both countries, performance effects on CEO or top director turnover are of the same order of magnitude as equivalent effects in the USA.

Having discovered that managerial pay and job security are related to recent performance, do we have any evidence that performance is actually improved because of this association? Here, the evidence is very thin. Abowd (1990) and Leonard (1990) both investigate this question, with mixed results. Abowd focuses on the issue of whether changes in the sensitivity of pay to performance influence subsequent performance. The answer appears to be yes for stockmarket performance measures and no for accounting indicators.

Another approach to this question is to investigate the relationship between management ownership of stock and company performance, since such ownership will automatically imply a strong relationship between performance and managerial reward. Unfortunately, substantial managerial ownership of equity in a company will also induce protection against takeover, so the managers who own substantial portions of equity can safely take some of their rewards on the golf course without fear for their jobs. The evidence reflects the interplay of these opposing forces. In the United States, the focus has been on the relationship between market valuation and managerial ownership of shares. This appears to be highly non-linear. For example, Morck et al. (1988) find that the relationship is positive for management ownership between 0 and 5 per cent, negative between 5 and 25 per cent and positive thereafter. The results for the UK reported in Curcio (1992) are exactly the reverse, that is, negative, positive, negative. However, Curcio goes on to look at total factor productivity performance and finds a weak positive relation between total factor productivity growth and management ownership of equity, for management stakes above 5 per cent.

Overall, therefore, the evidence as to whether management incentive structures actually work is very thin. Part of the problem is that much of the analysis is static whereas we know that, in practice, career concerns, promotion prospects and the like can generate very important incentive mechanisms. The obvious mechanism is to reward good performance by promotion and increased pay. The difficulty arises in actually isolating and measuring good performance. Furthermore, with regard to promotion, it is typically relative performance that matters. So, for the individual, it is just as good to take an action to reduce the measured performance of competing managers by one unit as to increase his own performance by one unit. If company performance as a whole depends on some degree of cooperation between managers, incentive structures of this kind can easily cause problems.

Do we have any evidence on the impact of different types of promotion and pay structures on performance? The answer, basically, is no. We know a fair bit about what things are like (see Main et al., 1993, for example) but little about what things work.[3] So, to summarize, we observe some relationship between managerial pay and the absolute and relative performance of companies in both type I and type II systems. What we do not know is how useful managerial incentive pay structures are in improving corporate performance and in aligning managerial objectives with those of the shareholders.

## 3 INTERNAL CONTROL: INDEPENDENT DIRECTORS

As before, the main problem to be overcome is the informational asymmetry between managers and the owners of the company. In type I systems, considerable use is made of independent (USA) or non-executive (UK) directors whose role is to undertake informed monitoring of management on behalf of the shareholders. Yet, in Britain, for example, non-executive directors are full members of the board of directors and are equally responsible (in law) for the management of the company as executive directors. How this management responsibility can be reconciled with the monitoring role is not clear. What is the incentive for the non-executive to perform this monitoring role? Again it is not clear. Suppose the management of a company is performing badly. Will the non-executives know? There is no guarantee that they will have the information. Suppose they do know. Why should they make a fuss rather than keep quiet and collect their fees? The only incentive, aside from loss of reputation, is that they may face legal retribution if things go badly wrong. This may well be a highly significant factor in the United States but much less so in Britain. And they have plenty of incentives for keeping quiet, given that non-executives are chosen by executive directors, owe their salary to executives and typically share many social and business connections with executives. Indeed, most non-executives are executive directors of other companies.[4] So too much should not be expected from independent directors, particularly in Britain.

Is there any evidence on their effectiveness? Hill and Snell (1988) indicate that shareholder weakness tends to be associated with a poorer acquisition strategy and less innovation. This relationship is unaffected by the number of outside directors on the board. On the other hand, Weisbach (1988) finds that, controlling for ownership structure, industry and size, the more important are outside directors, the stronger is the association between prior (inferior) performance and the probability that the CEO will resign. In other words, independent directors are useful in forcing out ineffective CEOs. Aside from these results there is little beyond the anecdotal, although the story, related by Davis and Kay (1990), of Dennis Stevenson's leadership of a non-executive coup against Tony Berry, the chairman and chief executive of Blue Arrow, illustrates just how difficult and expensive it is for non-executives who really wish to do something about poor management.

Overall, therefore, we cannot expect too much from independent directors in exercising control over managers. Generally speaking, they have neither the incentives nor the knowledge to make a good job of such a role.

## 4 EXTERNAL CONTROL: INSTITUTIONAL SHAREHOLDERS AND BANKS

In both type I and type II systems, large financial organizations hold substantial portions of the equity of most major companies. The difference between the systems in practice is that these organizations have some long-term commitment to the companies in the type II system but not in the type I system. In the type I system, the main equity holders are pension funds and other institutional shareholders, whereas in the type II system banks either hold or control substantial tranches of equity.

## Institutional shareholders

In the type I system, a typical institutional shareholder is a pension fund or unit trust which will be operating an actively managed portfolio. The relationship between these institutions and the companies in which they possess large equity holdings is generally 'arm's length'. Thus, for example, the survey evidence reported in Cosh et al. (1990) suggests that institutional investors carry out very little monitoring. This is justified by the fact that the financial institution has no expertise in running the sorts of businesses in which it invests and it cannot be privy to information which is not available to the generality of shareholders (because of insider trading regulations). In any event, any kind of close relationship would be more or less incompatible with active portfolio management (churning).

This is not to say that, from time to time, institutional shareholders, either individually or collectively, do not exert some direct influence on management.[5] For example, if companies want to come to the market with rights issues, the institutions have considerable leverage at this juncture and sometimes use it to impose management changes. More generally, institutions can, and sometimes do, express views on boardroom questions like management contracts, whether or not the offices of chairman and chief executive should be combined and similar issues. Overall, however, the standard institutional response to bad management is to treat it like any other feature of a company which influences decisions to buy, hold or sell.

## The role of banks

In the type II system, banks tend to have long-term relationships with companies and also to help in the provision of long-term capital. To what extent should we, therefore, expect banks to act in the interests of equity holders and to assist in the alignment of managerial objectives with those of the firm's owners? Consider, first, the incentives facing the banks. If banks only provide debt finance, it is not clear why they have any particular incentive to prevent non-present value maximizing behaviour by the management even if they have the power to do so. Of course, they face the risk of non-repayment of loans because of bankruptcy, but this sanction applies equally to the managers themselves, for whom the costs of bankruptcy are considerable. This suggests that in any effective bank monitoring system the banks should hold some equity, and this is typically the case in both Germany and Japan.

Of course, even if they hold equity, this will not ensure that the managers of the bank will act in the best interests of the shareholders of the companies whose equity they hold. The managers at the bank may have objectives which are at variance with those of shareholders even though the bank has an equity holding. This is simply because there may be no effective monitoring of their behaviour on behalf of the shareholders of the bank. For example, a director of the bank may assist the management of a company in which it has an equity holding to indulge in expensive acquisitions because this will increase the power and status of both the company management *and* the bank director, who is probably on the supervisory board of the company. In other words, unless the bank's shareholders can effectively monitor *their* managers, there is no guarantee that bank monitoring will be effective.[6] In fact, what happens in both Germany and Japan is that the banks typically only involve themselves seriously in the day-to-day activities of the company when things go wrong. In Germany they do this via their representation on the supervisory board whereas in Japan they simply appoint additional directors to represent their interests on the company board (see Lichtenberg and Pushner, 1992; Kaplan and Minton, 1993). When things are going well, however, the executive directors in both Japan and Germany operate with a very free hand.

One area where the close involvement of banks in the type II system does make a difference is in decisions about fixed capital investment. The evidence on this score provided by Cable (1985) and Hoshi et al. (1991) (see chapter 2, section 1) clearly indicates that bank involvement tends to improve investment decisions by removing asymmetries in information between managers and providers of funds.

## 5   OVERVIEW AND CONCLUSION

There are two distinct types of financial environment and modes of corporate governance. The type I system, exemplified by the USA or UK, has a large and efficient stockmarket with the majority of the equity in major companies under the control of shareholders who are not closely involved with the firm. In the type II system, exemplified by Japan and Germany, substantial portions of the equity in each company are under the control of shareholders who have some degree of long-term commitment to the firm.

What can we conclude about the workings of the two systems?

1   In the type I system, the existence of hostile takeovers may perhaps help to prevent gross managerial inefficiency. However, the typical hostile target is not a very badly performing company and, overall, the hostile takeover is a very crude and expensive activity.

2   Agreed mergers and takeovers are common in both type
    I and type II systems. In the type I system there is strong
    evidence that managers can and often do engage in
    acquisition strategies which are against the interests of
    shareholders. However, there is no evidence that type
    II systems militate against this activity.

3   Internal control in both type I and type II systems is
    provided by various incentive mechanisms which
    loosely relate managers' pay and job security to com-
    pany performance. The relationships between pay and
    performance appear not to differ greatly under the two
    systems. In the type I system, internal control is also
    provided via independent directors but this seems
    generally to be ineffective.

4   External control in the type II system is generally oper-
    ated via banks who either are, or represent, long-term
    shareholders. This helps with fixed capital investment
    decisions, but otherwise appears to have little impact
    on the firm unless things are going wrong. This method
    of operation appears to avoid some of the problems of
    short-termism apparent in the type I model.

Overall, therefore, while the type I system has some serious problems, which we set out in chapter 2, it is by no
means clear that the type II model represents a vastly
superior framework of corporate control. It has certain
advantages as we have seen, but in no sense can it be said
to explain the spectacular industrial success of Japan, in
particular.

In fact, the Japanese system is much more complex than
one in which banks monitor managers on behalf of shareholders. Indeed, as one expert commentator remarks, 'What
is striking about the Japanese system is the marked lack of
accountability that managers have to their shareholders'
(Odagiri, 1991, p. 27). In the Japanese system managers
make a large investment in the work force. Thus, as Ronald

Dore notes, in Japan 'managers see their primary duty not as being to their shareholders but rather to their employees' (Dore, 1991, p. 38). This induces a long-term relationship and a reciprocal commitment by the workforce to the company. This tends to force a long-term view on the management in order that the company may grow and enable managers to fulfil their commitments to the workforce. The role of the shareholders in all this is essentially passive, although whether it would remain passive if the shareholder rewards were not so substantial is another story.

In addition, it is clear that in the successful Japanese industries managers are constrained by the intense domestic competition. As Porter (1990) notes, a key feature of all the internationally successful Japanese industries is that they are the ones where domestic competition is at its fiercest. Conversely, those Japanese industries which are not internationally competitive are precisely those where domestic competition is feeble. This suggests that there is another important aspect to managerial decision making and corporate performance which we have yet to discuss, namely the role of competition. Does competition improve the performance of managers and companies? This is the topic of our next chapter.

## NOTES

1   In fact, in the most general models, it cannot even be demonstrated that the optimal reward is everywhere nondecreasing in the profit (see Grossman and Hart, 1983).
2   Rosen argues that log rather than arithmetic differences are superior because the latter are dominated by large firms and the arithmetic effect is expected to diminish for large firms because the risks are greater.
3   Tournament rewards do seem to have a positive impact on performance in professional golf tournaments (see Ehrenberg and Bognanno, 1990).

4  Davis and Kay (1990) report that in the 74 private sector quoted companies in the top 100 of the Times 1000 index, some 62 per cent of non-executive directors are executive directors of other companies.

5  Jenkinson and Mayer (1992) suggest that there is more evidence of an association between poor corporate performance and direct institutional intervention than between poor performance and hostile takeovers. This, however, has more to do with the particularly low association in the latter case rather than a particularly strong association in the former.

6  For example, the fact that Deutsche Bank held over 28 per cent of the equity of Daimler-Benz did not prevent the latter making a series of unrelated acquisitions of doubtful value to the shareholders in the mid to late 1980s (see section 2 chapter 2 for more details).

REFERENCES

Abowd, J. (1990) Does performance based management compensation affect corporate performance? *Industrial and Labor Relations Review*, 43(3), 52S–73S.

Antle, R. and Smith, A. (1986) An empirical investigation of the relative performance evaluation of corporate executives. *Journal of Accounting Research*, 24(2), 1–32.

Asquith, D., Opler, T. C. and Weston, J. F. (1990) The size and distribution of shareholder wealth gains from mergers: evidence from the takeover boom of the 1980s. UCLA Program in Applied Econometrics D.P. No. 11.

Barro, J. R. and Barro, R. J. (1990) Pay, performance and turnover of bank CEOs. *Journal of Labor Economics*, 8, 448–81.

Cable, J. (1985) Capital market information and industrial performance: the role of West German banks. *Economic Journal*, 95, 118–32.

Cosh, A., Hughes, A., Singh, A., Carty, J. and Plender, J. (1990) Takeovers and short-termism in the UK. IPPR Industrial Policy Paper No. 3.

Coughlin, A. T. and Schmidt, R. (1985) Executive compensation, management turnover, and firm performance: an empirical investigation. *Journal of Accounting and Economics*, 7(2), 43–66.

Curcio, R. (1992) Managerial ownership of shares and corporate performance: an empirical analysis of UK companies 1972–1986. London School of Economics, Centre for Economic Performance Working Paper No. 290.

Davis, E. and Kay, J. (1990) Corporate governance, takeovers and the role of the non-executive director. *Business Strategy Review*, 1, Autumn, 17–36.

Dore, R. (1991) R. and D. and innovation: lessons from Japan. In J. Philpott (ed.), *Improving Britain's Industrial Performance*. London: Employment Institute.

Ehrenberg, R. and Bognanno, M. (1990) Do tournaments have incentive effects? *Journal of Political Economy*, 98, 1307–27.

Franks, J. R. and Mayer, C. (1992) Hostile takeovers in the UK and the correction of managerial failure. Institute of Finance and Accounting Working Paper No. 156–92, London Business School, London.

Gibbons, R. and Murphy, K. J. (1990) Relative performance evaluation for chief executive officers. *Industrial and Labor Relations Review*, 43(3), 30S–51S.

Grossman, S. J. and Hart, O. D. (1980) Takeover bids, the free-rider problem and the theory of the corporation. *Bell Journal of Economics*, 11, 42–64.

Grossman, S. and Hart, O. (1983) An analysis of the principal agent problem. *Econometrica*, 51, 7–45.

Hill, C. W. L. and Snell, S. A. (1988) External control, corporate strategy, and firm performance in research intensive industries. *Strategic Management Review*, 9, 577–90.

Hoshi, T., Kashyap, A. and Scharfstein, D. (1991) Corporate structure, liquidity and investment: evidence from Japanese industrial groups. *Quarterly Journal of Economics*, 106, 33–60.

Jarrell, G. A., Brickley, J. A. and Netter, J. M. (1988) The market for corporate control: the empirical evidence since 1980. *Journal of Economic Perspectives*, 2, Winter, 49–68.

Jenkinson, T. and Mayer, C. (1992) *Hostile Takeovers*. London: Macmillan.

Jensen, M. C. and Murphy, K. J. (1990) Performance pay and top-management incentives. *Journal of Political Economy*, 98(2), 225–64.

Kaplan, S. N. (1992) Top executive rewards and firm performance: a comparison of Japan and the US. NBER Working Paper No. 4065, Cambridge, MA.

Kaplan, S. N. (1993) Top executives, turnover and firm performance in Germany. NBER Working Paper No. 4416, Cambridge, MA.

Kaplan, S. N. and Minton, B. A. (1993) Outside intervention in Japanese companies: its determinants and its implications for managers. NBER Working Paper No. 4276, Cambridge, MA.

Leonard, J. S. (1990) Executive pay and firm performance. *Industrial and Labor Relations Review*, 43(3), 13S–29S.

Lichtenberg, F. and Pushner, G. (1992) Ownership structure and corporate performance in Japan. NBER Working Paper No. 4092, June, Cambridge, MA.

Main, B. G. M. (1991) Top executive pay and performance. *Managerial and Decision Economics*, 12, 219–29.

Main, B. G. M., O'Reilly C. A. and Wade, J. (1993) Top executive pay: tournament or teamwork. *Journal of Labor Economics*, 11(4), 606–28.

Martin, J. and McConnell, J. (1991) Corporate performance, corporate takeovers and management turnover. *Journal of Finance*, 46, 671–87.

Morck, R., Shleifer, A. and Vishny, R. W. (1988) Management ownership and market valuation. *Journal of Financial Economics*, 20, 293–315.

Murphy, K. J. (1985) Corporate performance and managerial remuneration. *Journal of Accounting and Finance*, 7(2), 11–42.

Murphy, K. J. (1986) Incentives, learning and compensation: a theoretical and empirical investigation of managerial labour contracts. *Rand Journal of Economics*, 17(2), 59–76.

Nalebuff, B. and Stiglitz, J. (1983) Information, competition and markets. *American Economic Review, Papers and Proceedings*, 73, 278–83.

Odagiri, H. (1991) The interaction of growth and competition: the key to understanding Japanese management. *Business Strategy Review*, 2, Autumn, 25–37.

Porter, M. (1990) *The Competitive Advantage of Nations*. London: Macmillan.

Rosen, S. (1990) Contracts and the market for executives. NBER Working Paper No. 3542, Cambridge, MA.

Shleifer, A. and Vishny, R. W. (1988) Value maximization and the acquisition process. *Journal of Economic Perspectives*, 2, Winter, 7–20.

Warner, J. B., Watts, R. L, and Wruck, K. H. (1988) Stock prices, event prediction and event studies: an examination of top management changes. *Journal of Financial Economics*, 20(1/2), 461–92.

Weisbach, M. (1988) Outside directors and CEO turnover. *Journal of Financial Economics*, 20, 431–60.

# 4

# Competition and Corporate Performance

## INTRODUCTION

There is a widespread belief that competition improves the performance of companies. As Richard Caves remarks, economists have a 'vague suspicion that competition is the enemy of sloth' (Caves, 1980, p. 88). While standard economic theory indicates that competition leads to allocative efficiency by forcing prices to equal marginal costs, the general view is that competition has a much wider impact. To be more explicit, it is thought by many to exert downward pressure on costs, reduce slack, provide incentives for the efficient organization of production and drive forward innovation. However, this view is not totally accepted. An alternative, very loosely based on Schumpeter (1943), is the notion that market power is a prerequisite for innovation.[1] Arguably, this is the wrong way round. Firms facing fierce competition endlessly strive for competitive advantage. Hence they invest to reduce the level of competition, at least in the short run. They do this by innovating in ways which it is hard to copy quickly and, if they are successful, they generate some temporary market power. Nevertheless, it is competition in the broadest sense which pushes firms to seek such competitive advantage.

The purpose of this chapter is to investigate two questions on this general theme. First, how might competition improve corporate performance? Second, is there any evidence that it does? In particular, does competition induce managers to pursue the right strategies?

## 1   How Does Competition Work?

We take an industry to be more competitive if there are fewer monopoly rents. Our direct concern is with the impact of competition on the performance of companies. This is a perfectly legitimate issue to investigate, but care must be exercised because the degree of competition is not, in the long run, independent of company behaviour. Thus, for example, high performing companies may, eventually, gain a position of market power. This makes the interpretation of cross-section correlations very tricky.[2]

Bearing this in mind, why should competition influence the performance of companies? There are two possibilities we consider here. In the previous chapter, we noted that while Japanese managers appear to have few explicit incentives to align their objectives with those of the shareholders, they may yet perform well because of the degree of competition they face, which is intense in many Japanese industries and leaves no room for slack. So the first issue we investigate is how competition might improve managerial performance. The second is the relationship between competition and innovation.

Competition and managerial performance

The obvious way in which market power and managerial performance are related is that the existence of monopoly rents gives the company stakeholders, in particular managers and workers, the potential to capture these rents in the form of slack or lack of effort.

But this is simplistic. The owners of monopolistic firms will be just as keen to prevent slacking by managers and workers as the owners of competitive firms. However, it may be argued that the latter are in a better position to do so, at least under the uncontroversial assumption that mangers know more about what is going on than owners. Concerning managerial effort, the work of Holmstrom (1982a), Nalebuff and Stiglitz (1983) and Mookherjee (1984) suggests that explicit incentive schemes will generate sharper incentives the greater the number of players involved. This arises because of the greater opportunities for comparison of performance. Hart (1983) provides a model of managerial incentives which demonstrates explicitly how competition between firms may sharpen incentives. He supposes there to be two types of firm in an industry, 'managerial' (M), where there is a principal–agent problem, and 'entrepreneurial' (E), where the 'principal' runs the firm. All firms face common cost shocks. When (marginal) costs are low, E firms expand output whereas M firms have managers who take advantage of the good times to slack. This latter is consistent with their optimal incentive scheme under the condition that managers are not 'too responsive' to monetary incentives. If the proportion of E firms is higher, industry output in good times (low cost) is higher, industry prices are lower and the potential for managerial slack in the M firms is lower. This might be interpreted as an increase in competition leading to less slack. However, this is not a robust result. Scharfstein (1988) notes that the position is reversed if managers are highly

responsive to monetary incentives. Then 'competition' leads
to more slack.

An alternative analysis is based on an idea in Vickers
(1992) which utilizes a model of *implicit* rewards due to
Holmstrom (1982b). The idea is that while current managerial effort does not influence current earnings, it may influence future market-based rewards via its impact on the
market's estimate of the manager's ability. The market
cannot observe either effort or ability directly but in future
periods it can use knowledge of managerial output, which
depends on effort, ability and unobserved productivity
shocks. The manager, therefore, has an incentive to raise
effort early in her career because this will tend to increase
future market estimates of her ability, and hence future
rewards.

What is the role of competition in all this? Vickers's idea
is that the existence of other firms in the industry leads to
a sharpening of effort incentives because the unobserved
productivity shocks are likely to be correlated across firms
operating in the same industry. In Vickers (1992), he shows
that in a two-period model, first-period effort incentives
are greater when there are two firms, as long as the unobserved productivity shocks are more highly correlated across
the two firms than the unobserved managerial abilities, a
not unlikely scenario. This result can be extended to any
number of firms. To be more explicit, suppose there are
two periods, $n$ firms and in period $t$ the output of the
manager of firm $i$, $x_t^i$, is given by

$$x_t^i = a^i + e_t^i + u_t^i, \ t = 1, 2 \qquad (1)$$

where $a$ is the manager's ability, $e$ is the manager's effort
and $u^i$ is a productivity shock. The market observes only $x$
for each firm. The cost of effort to each manager is $c(e)$.
Since there are no *explicit* incentive payments, managerial
effort in period 2 is zero and the second period wage for

each manager is the market estimate of her ability. For the manager of firm 1, this is simply the expectation of $a^1$ conditional on the observed values of first period output in all the firms, that is $E[a^1 \mid x_1^1, \ldots, x_1^n]$. As long as the productivity shocks are correlated, output in every firm provides information about the productivity shock in firm 1 and hence about the ability of the manager. Her choice of effort in the first period depends on the extent to which an increase in her first period output, $x_1^1$, raises the conditional expectation of her ability. Under reasonable conditions, it may be shown that the more firms there are (the higher $n$), the more sensitive is the conditional expectation to first-period output. So with a greater number of firms in the industry, mangers have a greater incentive to provide effort in the first period because effort is more highly rewarded in terms of pay in the second period (see Nickell, 1993, appendix). Taking a rise in the number of firms to correspond to an increase in competition, this implies that competition can tend to raise managerial effort, and hence company performance.

An alternative framework relies not on the possibility of competition giving more precision to incentives based on relative performance but on the fact that competitive forces in the product market may raise the sensitivity of profits to the actions of managers. So if competition makes profits more responsive to managerial effort, for example, then owners have a greater incentive to ensure that managerial effort is kept high and inefficiency will be lower. Willig (1987) presents a model along these lines in which he demonstrates that in the context of a simple principal–agent framework, a *ceteris paribus* increase in the firm's product demand elasticity causes the firm's owners to induce the manager to raise her effort. However, a *ceteris paribus* fall in demand will have the opposite effect, so increased competition will only raise effort and efficiency if the demand elasticity effect dominates the demand reduction effect. Since an increase in competition may both raise the demand elasticity and reduce demand for the individual firm, the effort outcome is ambiguous. This demand reduction effect is central to the model in Martin (1995) and, with no offsetting elasticity effect, he obtains the unambiguous result that competition *reduces* managerial effort.

As well as managerial effort, competition may also influence the effort of workers. This follows naturally from the notion that product market rents may be shared with workers. Such sharing occurs because this makes the life of managers more comfortable (expense-preference, e.g. Smirlock and Marshall, 1983) or it enables unions to be kept out (e.g. Dickens and Katz, 1987), or already entrenched unions use their bargaining strength to enforce it (e.g. Stewart, 1990). Since rents may be captured in the form of higher wages or reduced effort, we have a direct connection between the degree of competition and the level of workers' effort. This result is particularly clear-cut in the bargaining model where unions and firms bargain over both wages and effort. In this case, increases in product market competition lead directly to increases in bargained effort (see Nickell, 1993, appendix).

So, to summarize, there is some theoretical basis for the belief that competition improves managerial performance (and, indeed, worker performance). But this theoretical foundation is not, as yet, very strong and some models generate results which point in the opposite direction.

## Competition and innovation

As we have already noted, there is a Schumpetarian viewpoint which indicates that competition and innovation do not go together. Larger and more monopolistic firms are more likely to undertake research and development (R and D) because they face less market uncertainty, have a larger and more stable cash flow, and can more easily appropriate the returns.

More formally, there are two opposing forces at work. The first works in favour of the view that competition leads to more innovation. Leaving aside strategic considerations, a competitive firm gains more from innovation than a monopoly. Consider a firm in a competitive industry making a homogeneous product such as cardboard. If this firm can find a cheaper method of making cardboard than any of its many competitors, it can 'scoop the pool'. In principle, it can take over the whole market and become a monopolist, an enormous reward compared to that which a monopolist in such an industry could gain by such a cost-reducing innovation. This is known as the *replacement effect* (due to Arrow, 1962). The opposing force arises from strategic considerations. Consider a monopolist relative to a potential entrant. By innovating, the monopolist can keep the potential entrant at bay and get to keep the monopoly position. The best the potential entrant can do by innovating is to gain admittance to what will then become a duopoly. But the profits of a monopolist are never less and usually greater than the joint profits of the duopolist. Thus, as Tirole (1989, p. 393) notes, 'because competition reduces profits, the monopolist's incentive to remain a monopolist is greater than the entrant's incentive to become a duopolist'. This is known as the *efficiency effect*.

The consequence of these opposing forces is that, in general, the relationship between competition (the number of firms) and R and D expenditure can be either positive or negative depending on the specification of the model. However, in the case of the search for a drastic innovation (e.g. winner takes all), the efficiency effect is irrelevant and the greater the number of firms, the bigger the prize and hence the greater the R and D intensity. Moreover, it is generally true that the expected time to a successful innovation decreases with the number of firms.

## Spillovers

Until now, we have ignored the very real possibility that innovations in one firm will spill over into other firms because it is hard to maintain secrecy and, even with patent protection, innovations can be copied. In any event, many valuable innovations cannot be patented (for example, new ways in which production is organized). Spillovers typically reduce the incentive to innovate because competitor firms will capture some of the benefits. This might reinforce the view that monopolies have greater incentives to innovate because they can appropriate all the gains, having no competitors. Porter (1990) strongly opposes this view, arguing that 'even though innovations are imitated, diffusion is incomplete and occurs with a lag' (p. 636). Furthermore, as is noted by Spence (1981), once there is an element of learning-by-doing in the innovations, then spillovers become less of a drawback and increased competition can easily result in better performance (see Carney, 1993, for an extensive analysis).

Overall, therefore, there is some theoretical foundation for the view that competition improves performance in both the static (efficiency) and dynamic (innovation) contexts. But the weight of the theoretical results is hardly overwhelming.

# 2  Does Competition Work?

What is the evidence on the role of competition in stimulating good performance in the corporate sector? First we shall look at the general evidence based on investigations of the direct impact of product market competition on company performance. Then we shall consider how competition influences management strategies to induce good performance. In particular we consider two types of management strategy, one dealing with the organization and structure of the company, the other with investment and innovations.

### General evidence on competition and company performance

Some of the most compelling evidence on the role of competition tends to be broad brush. For example, the very low level of productivity attained in Eastern Europe relative to Western Europe by the end of the Communist era is an impressive testament to what can be achieved by repressing competitive forces. More specifically, Porter (1990) demonstrates convincingly how domestic competition is a significant factor in generating world-beating industries. As he notes, 'Among the strongest empirical findings in our research is the association between vigorous domestic rivalry and the creation and persistence of competitive advantage in an industry' (p. 117). For example, he demonstrates that those areas of Japanese industry which are internationally successful are precisely those which have very high levels of domestic rivalry (a list may be found in Porter, 1990, table 8.3). Conversely, the large tracts of Japanese industry with little or no domestic competition contain no international success stories (e.g. construction, agriculture, food, paper, commodity chemicals). A third area of compelling general evidence is provided by the consequences of deregulation, which usually means an increase in competition. This generally leads to significant productivity gains in the firms affected (see Graham et al., 1983, on the US airline industry, for example).

What about more precise statistical evidence covering a wide range of sectors? Here we must distinguish between the effects of competition on *levels* of productivity or static efficiency, and on productivity *growth* or more general dynamic improvements. The best evidence is in the former area. For example, in recent years there have been a number of comprehensive studies of technical efficiency, which are reported in Caves and Barton (1990), Green and Mayes (1991) and Caves and associates (1992). These make use of frontier production function techniques to estimate technical efficiency indices and relate these to variables of interest. The relevant finding is that an increase in market concentration above a certain threshold tends to reduce technical efficiency. This result emerges in a number of countries and is consistent with the finding in the management literature, discussed in Caves (1980, pp. 85–6), that competition leads to companies employing more efficient decision making structures.

These are, of course, cross-section studies and, as such, are prone to omitted variable problems. However, their results tend to be confirmed in panel data studies on industries (Haskel, 1990) or firms (Nickell et al., 1992). In both examples a fixed effects framework is used to discover that market concentration (Haskel) or market share (Nickell) has an adverse effect on the *level* of (total factor) productivity. By the nature of the fixed effects estimation procedure, what this means in practice is that an increase in market concentration or market share is followed by a *ceteris paribus* fall in productivity. This view relates the result to the observation by the MIT commission in the USA (Dertouzos et al., 1989) that plants at the top of the productivity distribution sometimes rest on their laurels and lose their competitive advantage.[3]

Turning to evidence of competition effects on productivity *growth*, results are very thin on the ground. The problem is that the analysis tends to be cross-sectional and productivity growth performance is influenced by so many factors which are hard to capture and vary systematically across firms or industries. Furthermore, there is a problem of reverse causality; that is, firms with relatively high rates of productivity growth will tend to increase their market dominance. However, this latter point does at least push the correlation in the opposite direction to the one we seek, so if we can find a negative *ceteris paribus* correlation between productivity growth and market dominance, the reverse causality effect will ensure that this understates the true extent of the negative relationship. The only relevant result in the literature is in Nickell (1993), which notes that firms with more than five competitors tend to have higher rates of productivity growth, *ceteris paribus*, than the remainder.

## Competition and management strategies

What we are looking for is evidence that competition forces managers to undertake strategies which are known to improve performance. Some of the evidence is rather indirect. For example, it seems reasonable to suppose that competition reduces 'free cash flow'. And, as we have already seen in chapter 2 (p. 40), the existence of such free cash flow leads to wasteful practices on the part of managers (see Jensen, 1988). Another example is provided by Rhoades and Rutz (1982), who find that bankers who operate in a monopolistic market tend to reduce risks and lead a 'quieter life' than those who find themselves in a more competitive environment. However, there is a more specific strategy area where some evidence exists and that concerns the matching of the structure of the firm with its environment.

## The fit between structure and environment

Management organization theory puts some stress on the notion of a match between the structure of the firm and the environment in which it operates. The basic hypothesis is: the better the fit, the better the performance. So is there any evidence that competition leads to a better fit or match?

In order to investigate this question, we must go back a little. In the organization theory tradition, Woodward (1965) proposes that there should be some degree of fit between organization and technology. Thus she hypothesises that a mass production technology requires a high degree of centralization and formalization (well defined rules) whereas unit or batch production requires the reverse. Others, notably Burns and Stalker (1961), posit a relationship between firm structure and environmental uncertainty, with greater uncertainty being associated with lower levels of centralization and formalization (or a more 'organic' as opposed to 'mechanistic' structure). Much effort has been devoted to investigating the hypothesis that a better match, in one of the above senses, leads to better performance. Extensive investigations by Child (1974, 1975), Penning (1975) and Mohr (1971) have come up with very little hard evidence. Indeed, Penning concludes that 'The goodness of fit between environmental and structural variables has little bearing on the effectiveness of the organization.'

However, there is another aspect of organization whose relationship with corporate strategy does appear to be important, namely the adoption of the divisional structure (or M form) in response to increasing size *and* diversification. This view is espoused by Chandler (1966), whose basic hypothesis is that a strategy of diversification leads to the adoption of the divisional structure. This is done to offset the control loss arising in a monolithic structure producing a wide variety of different products. It is far better, it is claimed, to have each separate product or product group produced in its own division, with the head of each division being responsible to top management (see Williamson, 1981). Relating to this view are three hypotheses of interest. First, does diversification tend to lead to the adoption of the divisional structure? Second, do firms which diversify and have the divisional structure perform better than firms which diversify and don't have this structure? Third, does competition increase the incentive for firms which diversify to adopt the divisional structure?

With regard to the first hypothesis, the answer appears to be yes. Both Mahoney (1992) and Hamilton and Shergill (1992) present extensive evidence which demonstrates that diversification tends to lead to divisional structures. Evidence on the second is a little more mixed, for while Donaldson (1987) and Hamilton and Shergill (1992) find strong evidence in favour, Grinyer et al. (1980) find no evidence that diversification and performance are positively correlated among divisionalized companies (although they do find that, among non-divisionalized companies, diversification and performance are negatively related). Finally, with regard to the third hypothesis, Donaldson (1987) finds strong evidence in favour. In particular he finds that if there is a misfit between diversification strategy and structure, a more competitive environment causes there to be a relatively much poorer performance, thereby generating the incentive for a rapid adjustment of the structure in the direction of a good fit. Thus competition provides the incentive for a more rapid correction of the inferior (misfit) strategy.

## Competition and innovation

Porter (1990) is quite clear that competition leads to a high rate of innovation. Nowhere, he argues, is this more transparent than in Japan, where the innovative industries are marked by intense competition and a domestic customer base which tends to be both 'fickle' and very responsive to new products. Given the strong management focus on market share, this generates an enormous rate of innovation. This contrasts strongly with the feeble innovation performance in the Japanese sectors where domestic rivalry is all but absent.

Is there any more direct evidence? Unfortunately, while

there has been a great deal of cross-section econometric analysis of the relationship between market structure and innovative activity, most of this is uninformative. A typical empirical result is that innovative effort and output in an industry have an inverted U-shaped relationship with concentration. Levin et al. (1985), for example, find that industry innovation is at a maximum when the four-firm concentration ratio is 0.54. Two points are worth making about results of this type. First, while this cross-section relationship exists, it is not very important (Cohen and Levin, 1989). For example, Scott (1984) finds that while concentration and its square explain around 1.5 per cent of the variance of R and D expenditures across companies, two-digit industry dummies explain some 32 per cent. This relates to the second point, that in the cross-section industry studies there is inadequate control for technological opportunities, which tend to be both industry specific and correlated with market concentration.[4] So their omission will totally distort the true relationship between competition and innovation. In one study which avoids this problem,[5] namely Geroski (1990), the result is clear that concentration and other measures of market power tend to be associated with *lower* rates of innovation and productivity growth.

## Evidence on spillovers

As we have already seen, there is a *prima facie* case for the view that spillovers will reduce the incentive to innovate, particularly in a more competitive environment. So what do we know? First, it is clear that spillovers are important. In a wide-ranging survey, Griliches (1991) cites a variety of evidence on the significance of spillovers and concludes that (a) R and D spillovers are present, (b) their magnitude may well be large and (c) social rates of return to R and D are significantly above private rates. Second, there is some evidence that spillovers are stronger, the closer the physical proximity. Thus, Henderson (1986) finds that output per man hour is higher, *ceteris paribus*, in firms that have other firms in the same industry located nearby.[6] More convincingly, Jaffe et al. (1992) find that spillovers, as measured by patent citations (excluding self cites), are quite strongly localized and that the extent of geographic localization fades only slowly through time.

In the light of these externalities, we might expect to find that competition leads to a reduction in innovation because of weakening incentives. Porter (1990) argues against this, suggesting that his researches indicate that local competition appears to overcome the externality problem while taking full advantage of the extensive spillovers arising because of physical proximity. This possibility that free-rider problems can be overcome in a geographically close-knit business community, perhaps because it is socially unacceptable or because of cooperative monitoring, is not totally far-fetched. For example, German companies provide extensive general training to their younger employees and suffer very little poaching, at least partly because of the monitoring activities of local chambers of commerce (see Soskice, 1992).

An alternative, although related, view comes from Jacobs (1969), who believes that important knowledge spillovers come from outside the industry, although she agrees with Porter on the role of local competition. Direct evidence on this question is hard to come by although some results in Glaeser et al. (1991) are relevant. They consider a cross-section of city industries in the United States and, on the basis of their analyses of industry growth rates, conclude that competition is important, rejecting the view that local monopolies perform better because they enable the spillovers to be internalized. They also stress the role of industrial diversity as emphasized by Jacobs. Unfortunately, growth is measured by employment, which somewhat reduces the reliability of the results.

# 3 OVERVIEW AND CONCLUSION

1 There is a widespread belief that competition improves company performance. There is some theoretical basis for this belief (see points 2 and 3 below) but it is not very strong.

2 Competition may sharpen managerial incentives by enabling owners to compare the performance of many managers within the same industry or by raising the sensitivity of profits to managerial actions.

3 Competition may encourage innovation and long-term growth because innovation is more rewarding in a competitive framework.

4 There is some detailed evidence that competition is associated with higher *levels* of productivity. However, there is only a little evidence that it generates higher productivity growth.

5 There is some evidence that competition improves management strategies, in particular generating higher rates of innovation.

## NOTES

1 Schumpeter (1943) was clear that, in order to induce firms to undertake R and D, they must have the prospect of some degree of monopoly over the outcome. This does not mean that they must have monopoly power in general, although he does argue that some degree of size is helpful.

2 This is closely related to the discussion in Demsetz (1973).

3 This result is not, however, confirmed by Baily (1992).

4 For example, in the simple Dasgupta and Stiglitz (1980) framework, technological opportunities are captured by the elasticity of cost reduction with respect to R and D

expenditure. In equilibrium, this parameter is positively correlated with both R and D intensity and market concentration.

5   Geroski (1990) uses panel data and is able to absorb technological opportunities into industry fixed effects.

6   Although this could easily be due to an increase in the specialization and sophistication of the labour pool, a different kind of externality.

## REFERENCES

Arrow, K. (1962) Economic welfare and the allocation of resources for inventions. In R. Nelson (ed.), *The Rate and Direction of Inventive Activity*. Princeton, NJ: Princeton University Press.

Baily, M. N. (1992) Productivity dynamics in manufacturing plants. *Brookings Papers on Economic Activity, Microeconomics*, 187–249.

Burns, T. and Stalker, G. M. (1961) *The Management of Innovation*. London: Tavistock.

Carney, M. J. (1993) Competitive advantage and the advantage of competition: a theoretical analysis of national champions, learning-by-doing and spillovers. MPhil Thesis, St Peter's College, Oxford University.

Caves, R. (1980) Industrial organization, corporate strategy and structure. *Journal of Economic Literature*, 18, 64–92.

Caves, R. E. and Barton, D. R. (1990) *Efficiency in US Manufacturing Industries*. Cambridge, MA: MIT Press.

Caves, R. E. and associates (1992) *Industrial Efficiency in Six Nations*. Cambridge, MA: MIT Press.

Chandler, A. D. (1966) *Strategy and Structure: Chapters in the History of the Industrial Enterprise*. New York: Doubleday.

Child, J. (1974) Managerial and organizational factors associated with company performance, part I. *Journal of Management Studies*, 11, 175–89.

Child, J. (1975) Managerial and organizational factors associated with company performance, part II. *Journal of Management Studies*, 12, 12–27.

Cohen, W. M. and Levin, R. C. (1989) Empirical studies of innovation and market structure. In R. Schmalensee and R. D. Willig (eds), *Handbook of Industrial Organization*. Amsterdam: North-Holland.

Dasgupta, P. and Stiglitz, J. (1980) Industrial structure and the nature of innovative activity. *Economic Journal*, 90, 95–106.

Demsetz, H. (1973) Industry structure, market rivalry, and public policy. *Journal of Law and Economics*, 16, 1–10.

Dertouzos, M. L., Lester, P. K. and Solow, R. M. (1989) *Made in America: Regaining the Productive Edge*. Cambridge, MA: MIT Press.

Dickens, W. T. and Katz, L. F. (1987) Inter-industry wage differences and industry characteristics. In K. Lang and J. S. Leonard (eds), *Unemployment and the Structure of Labor Markets*. New York: Basil Blackwell.

Donaldson, L. (1987) Strategy and structural adjustment to regain fit and performance: in defence of contingency theory. *Journal of Management Studies*, 24, 1–24.

Geroski, P. (1990) Innovation, technological opportunity, and market structure. *Oxford Economic Papers*, 42, 586–602.

Glaeser, E. L., Kallal, H. D., Scheinkman, J. A. and Shleifer, A. S. (1991) Growth in cities. Santa Fe Institute Economics Research Program, Working Paper 91–09–036, Santa Fe Institute, NM.

Graham, D. R., Kaplan, D. P. and Sibley, D. S. (1983) Efficiency and competition in the airline industry. *Bell Journal of Economics*, 14, 118–38.

Green, A. and Mayes, D. (1991) Technical inefficiency in manufacturing industries. *Economic Journal*, 101, 523–38.

Griliches, Z. (1991) The search for R. and D. spillovers. NBER Working Paper 3768, July, Cambridge, MA.

Grinyer, P. H., Yasai-Ardekani, M. and Al-Bazzaz, S. (1980) Strategy, structure, the environment and financial performance in 48 United Kingdom companies. *Academy of Management Journal*, 23, 193–220.

Hamilton, R. T. and Shergill, G. S. (1992) The relationship between strategy–structure fit and financial performance in New Zealand: evidence of generality and validity with enhanced controls. *Journal of Management Studies*, 29, 95–113.

Hart, O. (1983) The market mechanism as an incentive scheme. *Bell Journal of Economics*, 14, 366–82.

Haskel, J. (1990) Imperfect competition, work practices and productivity growth. Economics Dept, Queen Mary and Westfield College, London, mimeo.

Henderson, J. V. (1986) Efficiency of resource usage and city size. *Journal of Urban Economics*, 19, 47–70.

Holmstrom, B. (1982a) Moral hazard in teams. *Bell Journal of Economics*, 13, 324–40.

Holmstrom, B. (1982b) Managerial incentive problems – a dynamic perspective. In *Essays in Economics and Management in Honor of Lars Wahlbeck*. Helsinki: Swedish School of Economics.

Jacobs, J. (1969) *The Economy of Cities*. New York: Vintage Books.

Jaffe, A. B., Trajtenberg, M. and Henderson, R. (1992) Geographic localization of knowledge spillovers as evidenced by patent citations. NBER Working Paper 3993, Cambridge, MA.

Jensen, M. C. (1988) Takeovers: their causes and consequences. *Journal of Economic Perspectives*, 2, Winter, 21–48.

Levin, R. C., Cohen, W. M. and Mowery, D. C. (1985) R and D appropriability, opportunity and market structure: new evidence on some Schumpeterian hypotheses. *American Economic Review, Papers and Proceedings*. 75, 20–4.

Mahoney, J. T. (1992) The adoption of the multidivisional form of organization: a contingency model. *Journal of Management Studies*, 29, 49–72.

Martin, S. (1995) Endogenous firm efficiency in a Cournot principal–agent models. *Journal of Economic Theory*, forthcoming.

Mohr, L. B. (1971) Organizational technology and organizational structure. *Administrative Science Quarterly*, 16, 444–59.

Mookherjee, D. (1984) Optimal incentive schemes with many agents. *Review of Economic Studies*, LI (3), 433–46.

Nalebuff, B. and Stiglitz, J. (1983) Prizes and incentives: towards a general theory of compensation and competition. *Bell Journal of Economics*, 14, 21–43.

Nickell, S. (1993) Competition and corporate performance.

Institute of Economics and Statistics, University of Oxford, mimeo.

Nickell, S. J., Wadhwani, S. and Wall, M. (1992) Productivity growth in UK companies, 1975–86. *European Economic Review*, 36, 1055–91.

Penning, J. (1975) The relevance of the structural-contingency model for organizational effectiveness. *Administrative Science Quarterly*, 20, 393–410.

Porter, M. (1990) *The Competitive Advantage of Nations*. London: Macmillan.

Rhoades, S. A. and Rutz, R. D. (1982) Market power and firm risk: a test of the quiet life hypothesis. *Journal of Monetary Economics*, 9, 73–85.

Scharfstein, D. (1988) Product market competition and managerial slack. *Rand Journal of Economics*, 36, 1055–91.

Schumpeter, J. (1943) *Capitalism, Socialism and Democracy*. London: Union University Books.

Scott, J. T. (1984) Firm versus industry variability in R. and D. intensity. In Z. Griliches (ed.), *R and D Patents and Productivity*. Chicago: University of Chicago Press.

Smirlock, M. and Marshall, W. (1983) Monopoly power and expense-preference behaviour: theory and evidence to the contrary. *Bell Journal of Economics*, 14, 166–78.

Soskice, D. (1992) The institutional infrastructure for international competitiveness: a comparative analysis of the UK and Germany. In A. B. Atkinson and R. Brunetta (eds), *The Economics of the New Europe*. International Economic Association Conference Series. London: Macmillan.

Spence, M. (1981) The learning curve and competition. *Bell Journal of Economics*, 12, 49–70.

Stewart, M. B. (1990) Union wage differentials, product market influences and the division of rents. *Economic Journal*, 100, 1122–37.

Tirole, J. (1989) *The Theory of Industrial Organization*. Cambridge, MA: MIT Press.

Vickers, J. (1992) Competition and implicit incentives. Seminar handout, Institute of Economics and Statistics, University of Oxford, mimeo.

Williamson, O. E. (1981) The modern corporation, origins, evolution, attributes. *Journal of Economic Literature,* 19, 1537–68.
Willig, R. D. (1987) Corporate governance and product market structure. In A. Razin and E. Sadka (eds), *Economic Policy in Theory and Practice.* London: Macmillan.
Woodward, J. (1965) *Industrial Organization: Theory and Practice.* London: Oxford University Press.

# 5

# Corporate Performance and the Labour Market

## INTRODUCTION

The employees of a company are one of its most important assets. How it makes use of these assets has an important bearing on performance and this will be our main topic of discussion in what follows. We begin by considering aspects of the labour market environment, notably the power of trade unions and the impact of employment protection legislation. Both of these have a significant effect on company behaviour and performance. We then go on to look at human resource strategies, in particular the impact of reward systems and employee participation on company performance. We conclude with some remarks on the relationship between participatory systems of management and the wider economic environment.

## 1 THE IMPACT OF TRADE UNIONS

Trade unions are not simply concerned with pay but have a significant effect on many areas of corporate life. In particular, they influence productivity, investment decisions with regard to both physical and human capital and, hence, profitability. Here we shall consider the evidence on these important topics.

### Pay

Unions tend to raise pay levels. The average union 'mark-up' based on cross-section data analysis is around 15 per cent in the United States (Lewis, 1986) and 8 per cent in the United Kingdom (Stewart, 1987). Estimates derived from panel data, where the measured mark-up is based on the *change* in an individual's pay consequent on a *change* in her union status, tend to be somewhat lower. However, when some effort is made to control for measurement error, the mark-up estimates are commensurate with the cross-section results (see Chowdhury and Nickell, 1985; Polachek et al., 1987).

These numbers are high enough to have a significant effect on companies. An 8 to 15 per cent increase in wage costs represents a considerable burden for the company concerned and might be thought to be enough to drive it out of business. However, the situation for companies is not as bad as might be expected. These average mark-ups mask large variations and the biggest mark-ups are associated with firms which face little competition. Indeed, Stewart (1990) finds that firms with many competitors typically exhibit no union mark-up at all unless most of their domestic competitors are also unionized and they face only weak foreign competition.

So the evidence suggests that union effects on pay reflect, in the main, the capture of monopoly rents. Rose (1987) calculates that the truckers were the 'dominant beneficiary' of the rents generated by trucking regulation in the United States. To conclude, union effects on wages are quite substantial and thus, potentially, highly distortionary. However these distortions are significantly attenuated to the extent that the high wages reflect the sharing of monopoly rents.

### Productivity and investment

It has been argued (Pencavel, 1977a; Freeman and Medoff, 1984) that the presence of unions can increase productivity because of their beneficial role in monitoring work and improving cooperation. On the other hand, their support of restrictive practices will clearly reduce productivity (Pencavel, 1977a). The balance of the evidence in both the USA and the UK favours the view that if unions have any impact on productivity, it is negative (for surveys of the evidence, see Hirsch and Addison, 1986, for the USA and Metcalf, 1990, for the UK). However, as with pay, there is again some evidence that the bigger effects are in those firms which enjoy some product market power (see Machin and Stewart, 1990; Conyon and Machin, 1991, for example). In other words, the adverse productivity effects tend to arise as a result of unions capturing monopoly rents in the form of indulgence in restrictive practices and other types of 'effort' reduction.

On the investment front, there are again opposing effects. On the plus side, if unions raise pay, this will put pressure on firms to invest more heavily so as to reduce their need for expensive labour. On the minus side, unions may actually inhibit new investment by insisting on inflexible work rules or firms may be deterred if they think that unions will capture some of the future quasi-rents. The evidence here is very mixed although the more reliable panel data results suggest that negative effects predominate (see Denny and Nickell, 1992, for example). On the other hand, it appears that both men and women in unionized workplaces receive more job-related training than their counterparts in non-union establishments (see Booth, 1991; Claydon and Green, 1992). So unions are good for investment in human capital.

Overall, therefore, unions tend to affect the performance of companies by raising pay and, in some cases, by lowering productivity and investment. However, these effects are strongly attenuated if the firm operates in a competitive environment. Unions are only likely to have serious effects on the performance of a company if it generates significant monopoly rents, for they seem adept at capturing them.

## 2    EMPLOYMENT PROTECTION

Employment protection legislation refers to those laws governing employment contracts, unfair dismissal and redundancy. Roughly speaking, these laws tend to raise the cost of employee separations initiated by the employer, thereby reducing employment flexibility. There are two aspects to this. First, the cost of firing incompetent or disruptive employees is increased. This will tend to make *hiring* more expensive as firms will have a greater incentive to spend resources on vetting and monitoring prospective employees. Second, the costs associated with redundancy or permanent layoff are higher, leading firms to use alternative methods of adjusting their labour input in slumps, by using short-time working, for example. The overall consequences of employment protection for companies are an enhanced role for the personnel function (see Daniel and Stilgoe, 1978, for strong evidence on this), a slower adjustment of employment in response to external shocks and an increase in average job tenures.

Evidence on the last two of these is clear-cut. Nickell (1979) and Burgess (1988) illustrate clearly how the introduction of employment protection legislation in Britain in the early 1970s led to companies adjusting employment more sluggishly in response to external shocks (and, incidentally, to an increase in cyclical fluctuations in working hours as a consequence). Cross-country comparisons confirm these results, with those countries with severe employment protection laws (like Italy) having much slower employment responses and longer job tenures than those without such laws, such as the United States (see Layard et al., 1991, chapter 9; Abraham and Houseman, 1993, for example).

While these influences on company behaviour are clear-cut, the overall impact of employment protection legislation on corporate performance is less clear. While very severe legislation may have serious consequences by greatly inhibiting flexibility, some degree of legislated employment protection may serve a useful purpose by encouraging firms to adopt a long-term strategy of investing in employees. In order to investigate this type of question, we must probe more deeply into the internal strategies of the firm with regard to its workforce.

## 3  REWARD SYSTEMS AND PERFORMANCE

Many systems of pay base part of employee compensation on something aside from time spent at work. The idea is to link pay, in some way or other, to performance. Performance, here, does not necessarily refer to the individual concerned but can refer to some entity of which she is part. This entity may be anything from a small group to the whole company. We have already discussed this issue with regard to managers, so here we shall be solely concerned with non-supervisory employees. In particular we shall analyse three types of reward system, namely individual incentive systems, group systems (e.g. gain sharing) and whole firm systems (e.g. profit sharing).

### Individual incentive schemes

Individual pay schemes may be divided into two types: those where individual output is easily measured in terms of units of product, and those where output is more nebulous and the scheme relies on the judgement of managers or supervisors.

The first type is known as the piece rate system, where individual workers are 'paid by the piece'. The evidence suggests the workers operating this system typically earn more and produce more output than those doing the same job on a straight time system (see, for example, King, 1975; Pencavel, 1977b; Seiler, 1984). This may, of course, be due to the fact that fast workers will naturally gravitate towards plants which operate piece rate systems. However, the system only works well, and is generally only applied, where the need for integration and cooperation among the workforce is negligible and the nature of the work is stable. Otherwise endless problems develop from the difficulties of pricing each job. As a consequence, the piece work system is not in widespread use. In the United States, for example, its use in manufacturing has been declining since the 1920s (see Mitchell et al., 1990, pp. 36–42; Brown, 1992) and by 1975 only around 1.2 per cent of US workers operated with this system (see Flaim, 1979, quoted in Bishop, 1987, p. 538).

The second type of pay system is known as performance-related pay or merit pay, where earnings are related to performance as assessed by superiors. Such pay systems are commonplace for white-collar workers but less so for blue-collar employees. For example, Casey et al. (1992) indicate that, in the UK, merit pay systems for white-collar workers operate in around 70 per cent of organizations, whereas for blue-collar workers the figure is less than half this number. The main problem with the system arises from the assessment mechanism. First, supervisory assessments are highly error prone. For example, King et al. (1980) indicate that the upper bound on the correlation between the ratings given to the same worker by two different raters is a mere 0.6. Furthermore, Hunter (1983) reports that the correlation between supervisor ratings and actual performance (using carefully designed work sample measures) is around 0.4 in studies of civilian jobs (it is only 0.27 in the military).

Second, because performance varies over time, but assessments are made at particular points, this further reduces the correlation between the assessment and average performance. Finally, the operators of the merit pay system often 'tone down' the impact of the assessments on pay in order to reduce unpleasantness and jealousy (see Brown, 1992). The consequence of all these difficulties with the assessment system is that the relationship between pay and the assessed level of productivity is typically only a very weak one (see Bishop, 1987).

In the light of this, what are the consequences of merit pay for performance? Pearce et al. (1985) find that the merit pay program in the US Social Security Administration had no effect on organizational performance. Marsden and Richardson (1992) echo this result in their study of performance pay in the UK Inland Revenue. They conclude that 'it is by no means implausible that the net motivational effect [of the introduction of the performance pay scheme] has been negative.' Finally, in a more wide-ranging study, Holzer (1990) finds that individual productivity scores and changes in these scores are *negatively* related to the existence of pay incentive schemes. So there is, as yet, no compelling evidence that merit pay systems actually work.

## Group incentive systems

Half-way between individual incentive schemes and profit sharing, we have collective bonus schemes based on the performance of a group, sector or department. In the United Kingdom, some 16–18 per cent of employers utilize such schemes for blue-collar workers (see Casey et al., 1992), although the number appears to be lower in the United States. The great advantage of group, as opposed to individual, incentive plans is that they encourage cooperation and mutual monitoring of performance within the group. The fundamental question is, does this outweigh the negative effects of the free-rider problem? The answer appears to be yes. The evidence from the United States seems to indicate that group incentive schemes lead to substantial increases in productivity. Thus, for example, Kaufman (1990) finds that in 112 companies which have introduced IMPROSHARE, a well-known gain sharing plan, the median productivity increase in the first year after introduction is 8 per cent. Furthermore, the increase continues in the second and third years, rising to a plateau at around 17.5 per cent. This positive view is confirmed in the evidence surveyed by Mitchell et al. (1990).

Why, if they work, do firms not make use of these schemes in far greater numbers? There are a number of possible reasons. First, the evidence may be misleading because firms may only introduce such schemes when they are in trouble and productivity improves as they get out of it (which they may well do anyway, without the scheme). Second, the introduction of group incentive schemes typically involves managerial effort and commitment. It may, also, involve some loss of managerial control as the groups typically want to have more say in how things are done. Third, the best performing workers may leave after the introduction of group incentives, since they will find that their high performance is not directly rewarded. This in fact happens, according to the evidence reported in Weiss (1987). Overall, however, the evidence suggests that group incentive schemes are more effective than individual ones.

## Company-wide incentives

Company-wide incentive systems usually involve some form of profit sharing or share ownership. Employee share ownership plans (ESOPs) obviously include an element of profit sharing in the sense that increased profits generally mean increased performance of the firm's equity. Furthermore, as Blasi (1990) points out, the vast majority (96 per cent) of profit-sharing schemes in the United States are, in fact, deferred profit-sharing trusts which involve substantial employee ownership of employer securities. Profit sharing and ESOPs are more common than group incentive schemes, with around 30 per cent of organizations making some use of profit sharing and around 20 per cent making use of ESOPs.

How do company-wide incentive schemes work? The free-rider problem is even more severe here than with group schemes and, at first sight, it appears unlikely that a share of the profits of a firm which employs 20 000 individuals on several sites, say, can have any impact on the behaviour of one particular individual. Nevertheless, the evidence suggests that company-wide incentive schemes do have a small but significant impact on the level of productivity. Thus Weitzman and Kruse (1990) summarize the results of a series of studies using some 42 different data sets, and conclude that profit sharing induces a median gain of 4.4 per cent in the level of productivity. Why this should be so is not clear, although it seems likely that profit sharing is associated with other participatory activities which might have positive productivity effects. However, Mitchell et al. (1990) indicate that even controlling for other economic and non-economic participating factors, profit sharing and

ESOPs have strong positive effects on productivity. Our next step, therefore, will be to analyse worker participation in more detail.

## 4    PARTICIPATION AND CORPORATE PERFORMANCE

Participation refers to the involvement of employees in the operation of a company. Levine and Tyson (1990) specify three types of participation. First is *consultative participation*, where employees give their opinions but management makes the decisions. Quality circles are a good example, where small groups of workers meet regularly to identify and discuss quality, productivity and other issues. Second is *substantive participation*, where employees are not only consulted but have some degree of autonomy in decision taking, as in work teams. Third is *representative participation*, which includes worker representation on committees all the way from joint consultative committees to the main board of directors. This is similar to consultative participation since workers are rarely a majority on any committee. They do, however, get to talk about a wider range of subjects.

The weight of the evidence suggests that substantive participation has a positive and significant impact on the level of productivity but that other types of participation have very little effect (see Mitchell et al., 1990; Levine and Tyson, 1990, table 1, for a valuable summary of the evidence). Not all authors agree with the latter point. Morishima (1991), for example, finds that, in Japan, information sharing via joint consultative committees (JCCs) both raises productivity and reduces unit costs. However, there is very little evidence *against* the view that substantive participation improves productivity performance.

Participation alone has an effect, but Levine and Tyson (1990) conclude, from their survey of the evidence, that its impact is greatly enhanced if it is accompanied by four other industrial relations characteristics. These are (a) profit sharing or some other group incentive scheme, (b) long-term employment relations and job security, (c) measures to build group cohesiveness and (d) a system of guaranteed employee rights. The fact that profit sharing fits with participation is hardly surprising. If participation requires some degree of effort from employees and leads to improved company performance, it is only natural that the employees should demand a share. The argument also goes through in reverse. A company which introduces profit sharing can expect demands for substantive participation. If an employee's pay is influenced by the performance of her company, she will expect some say in the decisions which affect that performance.

Some degree of job security is essential in any participatory scheme because no one is going to suggest, or cooperate in, efficiency improvements if her job is at risk as a consequence. Furthermore, substantive participation requires more (firm-specific) training and this is only worth providing if the employment relation is long term. The notion of group cohesiveness is an elusive one, but its most obvious aspect is the narrowing of pay and particularly status differentials (e.g. one canteen for all grades of employee). This would tend to increase trust between workers and management, and generally to increase cooperation. Finally, a system of guaranteed employee rights, particularly freedom from arbitrary dismissal, is essential for a participatory system. If employees have no rights, then they will never be in a position to talk openly because of the danger of reprisal. Under such circumstances, participation cannot work.

## How does participation work?

How does participation improve performance? There are two possibilities which are not mutually exclusive. First, there is a *cognitive aspect* to the process. That is, it works because it actually improves efficiency directly via the increased flow of information and knowledge in a participatory environment. Second, there is an *affective aspect*. Thus, it works because it leads to the attainment of higher order needs (respect, independence etc.), which imply increased morale and satisfaction leading to greater motivation and higher productivity. In a wide-ranging review of the literature based on over 60 studies, Miller and Monge (1986) conclude that there is some support for the cognitive aspect of the process *and* strong support for the affective aspect. So both are involved but the latter is, perhaps, more important. However, some of these results are disputed by Wagner and Gooding (1987).

## Participation and the Japanese system of management

The four concomitants of participation, which enhance its effectiveness, add up to something close to the Japanese management system. Such a system has a number of characteristics, notably: (a) a high level of worker responsibility and control, including, for example, responsibility for maintenance and quality control, and team-based production with rotation within and between teams; (b) strong incentives for both individual and group performance, including, for example, pay based on tenure *and* individual performance, large profit related bonuses, promotion from within the firm and long-term job security with guaranteed employee rights; (c) small numbers of job classifications and narrow differentials; (d) very extensive screening of prospective employees prior to hiring plus a great deal of training.

The evidence suggests both that these management practices, if they can be instituted, lead to high levels of productivity, and that the whole system can be operated successfully outside Japan, so it is not totally culture bound. For example, Hashimoto (1991) indicates that Japanese run automobile plants in the United States are at least as close in performance to Japanese automobile plants in Japan than they are to US run plants in the United States. For example, in table 1, we see this in terms of both productivity and quality. However, we also see, in the third row, the enormous investment in training required to make the Japanese system work.

So what characteristics of the external environment make it easier to adopt the Japanese system? Levine and Tyson (1990) provide the following list.

1  Small demand fluctuations.
2  Universal narrow wage dispersion.
3  Universal employment protection.
4  Long-term investor commitment.
5  High levels of general skill at the outset of an average working career.

The importance of each of the factors on this list is relatively clear. Small demand fluctuations make it much less expensive to sustain a long-term employment commitment. An alternative or complementary mechanism is for the firm to make extensive use of sub-contractors and casual employees, which gives it considerable flexibility in the face of demand variation. This is commonplace in Japan. The role of universal narrow wage dispersion is to reduce the poaching of good workers by outside firms. Universal employment protection, on the other hand, prevents firms offering long-term job security from falling foul of adverse selection problems. In a world where workers can be sacked at will, poor performers will automatically gravitate to the

**Table 1** Average characteristics of automobile plants in Japan and the USA

| | Japanese owned plants in Japan | Japanese owned plants in the USA | US owned plants in the USA |
|---|---|---|---|
| Hours of labour per car | 16.8 | 20.8 | 24.1 |
| Defects per 100 cars | 52.1 | 54.7 | 78.4 |
| Training hours per worker | 380 | 370 | 46 |

*Source:* Hashimoto, 1991

most secure environment, thereby raising the costs of screening prospective employees.

Long-term investor commitment is important because the high investment in specific human capital required by the system does not show up on the asset side of the balance sheet and this may, in the short run, give the appearance of weakness. In the longer term, of course, there is no problem. High levels of general skill on leaving full-time education are very important because this substantially reduces screening and training costs. Finally, it is worth remarking that the system seems to operate well whether or not the plant is unionized, as long as there is a single union.

## SUMMARY AND CONCLUSION

1    Trade unions raise pay, probably have a negative effect on productivity, possibly reduce fixed capital investment but appear to raise human capital investment. These effects typically reflect the capture of monopoly rents. The impact of unions is far less important where firms operate in a competitive environment.

2    Employment protection legislation reduces employment flexibility but encourages long-term employment relations and an enhanced personnel function.

3    Perhaps surprisingly, the evidence suggests that group-based reward systems have a bigger positive impact on productivity than individual-based systems. This may be because group systems tend to operate in a participatory environment which itself leads to improved productivity performance.

4    Participation, when it is substantive (i.e. involves employees in decision making as opposed simply to information sharing), has a positive impact on productivity. This effect is enhanced when it is associated with group-based reward systems, long-term employment relations,

measures to build group cohesiveness and guaranteed employee rights.

5   This last 'package' is close to the Japanese management system, which appears to generate very high levels of productivity and can be operated successfully outside Japan. The environment in which it operates best has small demand fluctuations, narrow wage dispersion, employment protection, long-term investor commitment and high levels of general skill generated by the schooling/training system.

## REFERENCES

Abraham, K. G. and Houseman, S. N. (1993) Does employment protection inhibit labor market flexibility? Lessons from Germany, France and Belgium. W. E. Upjohn Institute for Employment Research, Staff Working Paper No. 93–16.

Bishop, J. (1987) The recognition and reward of employee performance. *Journal of Labor Economics (the New Economics of Personnel)*, 5, no. 4(2), S36–S56.

Blasi, J. R. (1990) Comment on Conte and Svejnar. In A. S. Blinder (ed.), *Paying for Productivity: a Look at the Evidence*. Washington, DC: The Brookings Institution.

Booth, A. (1991) Job-related formal training: who receives it and what is it worth? *Oxford Bulletin of Economics and Statistics*, 53, 281–94.

Brown, C. (1992) Pay and performance. University of Michigan, Ann Arbor, mimeo.

Burgess, S. (1988) Employment adjustment in UK manufacturing. *Economic Journal*, 98, 81–103.

Casey, B., Lakey, J. and White, M. (1992) Payment systems: a look at current practice. UK Employment Department, Research Series Paper No. 5.

Chowdhury, G. and Nickell, S. (1985) Hourly earnings in the United States: another look at unionization, schooling, sickness and unemployment using PSID data. *Journal of Labor Economics*, 3, 38–69.

Claydon, T. and Green, F. (1992) The effect of unions on training provision. Dept of Economics, Leicester University, DP92/3, January.

Conyon, M. and Machin, S. (1991) The determination of profit margins in UK manufacturing. *Journal of Industrial Economics*, 39, 369–82.

Daniel, W. W. and Stilgoe, E. (1978) *The Impact of Employment Protection Laws*. London: Policy Studies Institute.

Denny, K. and Nickell, S. (1992) Unions and investment in British industry. *Economic Journal*, 102, 874–87.

Flaim, P. (1979) *Validation of Earnings Data Surveyed through Current Population Survey*. Washington, DC: US Department of Labor.

Freeman, R. and Medoff, J. (1984) *What Do Unions Do?* New York: Basic Books.

Hashimoto, M. (1991) Employment-based training in Japanese firms in Japan and in the United States: experiences of automobile manufacturers. Presented at the Conference on International Comparisons of Private Sector Training, 15–17 December, LSE. Ohio State University, mimeo.

Hirsch, B. and Addison, J. (1986) *The Economic Analysis of Unions*. London: Allen and Unwin.

Holzer, H. J. (1990) The determinants of employee productivity and earnings. *Industrial Relations*, 29, 403–22.

Hunter, J. E. (1983) A causal analysis of cognitive ability, job knowledge, job performance, and supervisor ratings. In F. Landy, S. Zedeck and J. Cleveland (eds), *Performance Measurement and Theory*. Hillsdale, NJ: Erlbaum.

Kaufman, R. T. (1990) The effects of IMPROSHARE on productivity. Smith College, Northampton, MA, mimeo.

King, L. M., Hunter, J. E. and Schmidt, F. L. (1980) Halo in a multidimensional forced choice performance scale. *Journal of Applied Psychology*, 65, 507–16.

King, S. L. (1975) Incentive and time pay in auto dealer repair shops. *Monthly Labor Review*, 98, 45–8.

Layard, R., Nickell, S. and Jackman, R. (1991) *Unemployment: Macroeconomic Performance and the Labour Market*. Oxford: Oxford University Press.

Levine, D. I. and Tyson, L. D'A. (1990) Participation, productivity and the firm's environment. In A. S. Blinder (ed.), *Paying for Productivity: a Look at the Evidence*. Washington, DC: The Brookings Institution.

Lewis, H. G. (1986) *Union Relative Wage Effects: a Survey*. Chicago: University of Chicago Press.

Machin, S. and Stewart, M. (1990) Unions and the financial performance of British private sector establishments. *Journal of Applied Econometrics*, 5, 327–50.

Marsden, D. and Richardson, R. (1992) Motivation and performance related pay in the public sector: a case study of the Inland Revenue. London School of Economics, Centre for Economic Performance D.P. No. 75.

Metcalf, D. (1990) Union presence and productivity levels, productivity growth and investment behaviour in British manufacturing industry. London School of Economics, Centre for Labour Economics Working Paper No. 1203.

Miller, K. I. and Monge, P. R. (1986) Participation, satisfaction and productivity: a meta-analytic review. *Academy of Management Journal*, 29, 727–53.

Mitchell, D. J. B., Levin, D. and Lawler, E. E. III (1990) Alternative pay systems, firm performance and productivity. In A. S. Blinder (ed.), *Paying for Productivity: a Look at the Evidence*. Washington, DC: The Brookings Institution.

Morishima, M. (1991) Information sharing and firm performance in Japan. *Industrial Relations*, 30, 37–61.

Nickell, S. J. (1979) 'Unemployment and the structure of labor costs. *Carnegie-Rochester Conference Papers on Public Policy*, 11, 187–222.

Pearce, J. L., Stevenson, W. B. and Perry, J. L. (1985) Managerial compensation based on organizational performance: a time series analysis of the effects of merit pay. *Academy of Management Journal*, 28, 261–78.

Pencavel, J. (1977a) Distributional and efficiency effects of trade unions in Britain. *British Journal of Industrial Relations*, 15, 137–56.

Pencavel, J. H. (1977b) Work effort, on-the-job screening, and alternative methods of remuneration. In R. G. Ehrenberg (ed.), *Research in Labor Economics, vol. 1.* Greenwich, CT: JAI Press.

Polachek, S., Wunnava, P. and Hutchins, M. (1987) Panel estimates of union effects of wages and wage growth. *Review of Economics and Statistics,* 69, 527–31.

Rose, N. (1987) Labor rent sharing and regulation: evidence from the trucking industry. *Journal of Political Economy,* 95, 1146–78.

Seiler, E. (1984) Piece rate vs. time rate: the effect of incentives on earnings. *Review of Economics and Statistics,* 66, 363–76.

Stewart, M. (1987) Collective bargaining arrangements, closed shops and relative pay. *Economic Journal,* 97, 140–56.

Stewart, M. (1990) Union wage differentials, product market influences and division of rents. *Economic Journal,* 100, 1122–37.

Wagner, J. A. III and Gooding, R. Z. (1987) Shared influence and organizational behaviour: a meta-analysis of situational variables expected to moderate participation–outcome relationships. *Academy of Management Journal,* 30, 524–41.

Weiss, A. (1987) Incentives and worker behaviour: some evidence. In H. R. Nalbantian (ed.), *Incentives, Cooperation and Risk Sharing: Economic and Psychological Perspectives on Employment Contracts.* Totowa, NJ: Rowman and Littlefield.

Weitzman, M. L. and Kruse, D. L. (1990) Profit sharing and productivity. In A. S. Blinder (ed.), *Paying for Productivity: a Look at the Evidence.* Washington, DC: The Brookings Institution.

# Stephen Nickell Publications

The Unemployment Crisis, Oxford University Press, 1994 (with R. Jackman and R. Layard).

Unemployment revisited. Journal of Economic Studies (NAIRU special issue), 20(1/2), 1993.

Cohort size effects on the wages of young men in Britain 1961–89. British Journal of Industrial Relations, September 1993.

An investigation into the power of insiders in wage determination. European Economic Review, December 1992 (with P. Kong).

The occupational success of young men who left school at sixteen. Oxford Economic Papers, July 1992 (with S. Connolly and J. Micklewright).

Unions and investment in British industry. Economic Journal, July 1992 (with K. Denny).

Productivity growth in UK companies. European Economic Review, 36, June 1992 (with S. Wadhwani and M. Wall).

*Unemployment: Macroeconomic Performance and the Labour Market.* Oxford University Press, 1991 (with R. Jackman and R. Layard).

Employment determination in British industry: investigations using micro-data. *Review of Economic Studies,* October 1991 (with S. Wadhwani).

Unions and investment in British manufacturing industry. *British Journal of Industrial Relations,* March 1991 (with K. Denny).

Mrs Thatcher's miracle? *Economic Affairs,* 10 January 1990 (with R. Layard).

Is unemployment lower if unions bargain over employment? *Quarterly Journal of Economics,* August 1990 (with R. Layard) (also in Y. Weiss and G. Fishelson (eds), *Advances in the Theory and Measurement of Unemployment,* Macmillan, 1990).

Turnover in UK manufacturing. *Economica,* August 1990 (with S. Burgess).

Inflation and the UK labour market. *Oxford Review of Economic Policy,* 8(4), 1990 (also in F. Hahn (ed.), *The Market, Practice and Policy,* Macmillan, 1992).

Insider forces and wage determination. *Economic Journal,* 100, June 1990 (with S. Wadhwani).

Unemployment: a survey. *Economic Journal,* 100, June 1990 (also in A. Oswald (ed.), *Surveys in Economics,* vol. 1, Basil Blackwell, 1991).

The real wage–employment relationship in the United States. *Journal of Labor Economics,* 8, January 1990 (with J. Symons).

*The Nature of Unemployment in Britain: Studies of the DHSS Cohort.* Clarendon Press, 1989 (with W. Narendranathan, J. Stern and J. Garcia).

Real wages and unemployment in Britain during the 1930s. *Economic Journal,* 99, June 1989 (with N. H. Dimsdale and N. Horsewood).

The Thatcher miracle? *American Economic Review,* 79, May

1989 (with R. Layard) (also in German translation in *Wirtschaft und Gesellschaft*, 15, 1989).

Wages and economic activity. In W. Eltis and P. Sinclair (eds), *Keynes and Economic Policy*, Macmillan, 1988.

Imperfect competition and the labour market. In M. Beenstock (ed.), *Modelling the Labour Market*, Chapman and Hall, 1988.

The supply side and macroeconomic modeling. In R. C. Bryant, D. W. Henderson, G. Holtham and S. A. Synansky (eds), *Empirical Macroeconomics for Interdependent Economies*, Brookings, 1988.

Unions, wages and employment. *European Economic Review*, 32(4), 1988 (with S. Wadhwani).

The short-run behaviour of labour supply. In T. Bewley (ed.), *Advances in Econometrics, Fifth World Congress*, Cambridge University Press, 1987.

The labour market. In R. Dornbusch and R. Layard (eds), *The Performance of the British Economy*, Clarendon Press, 1987 (with R. Layard).

*The Rise in Unemployment*, Basil Blackwell, 1987 (with C. Bean and R. Layard).

Unemployment and the real wage. In C.-H. Siven (ed.), *Unemployment in Europe*, Timbro, 1987.

A historical perspective on unemployment: a review article. *Journal of Political Economy*, August 1987.

*An Incomes Policy to Help the Unemployed*, Employment Institute, March 1987 (with R. Layard).

Why is wage inflation in Britain so high? *Oxford Bulletin of Economics and Statistics*, February 1987.

Estimating the parameters of interest in a job search model. In R. Blundell and I. Walker (eds), *Unemployment, Search and Labour Supply*, Cambridge University Press, 1986 (with W. Narendranathan).

Dynamic models of labour demand. In O. Ashenfelter and R. Layard (eds), *Handbook of Labor Economics*, North-Holland, 1986.

A disaggregated disequilibrium model of the labour market. *Oxford Economic Papers*, November 1986 (with M. Andrews).

Unemployment in Britain. *Economica* (special issue on unemployment), August 1986 (with R. Layard).

The rise of unemployment. A multi-country study. *Economica* (special issue on unemployment), August 1986 (with C. Bean and R. Layard).

The government's policy for jobs: an analysis. *Oxford Review of Economic Policy*, 1(2), 1985.

Modelling the process of job search. *Journal of Econometrics*, 28, 1985 (with W. Narendranathan).

An investigation into the incidence and dynamic structure of sickness and unemployment in Britain, 1965–75. *Journal of the Royal Statistical Society*, Series A, Part 3, 1985 (with W. Narendranathan and D. Metcalf).

Understanding unemployment. *Empirica* (*Austrian Economic Papers*), 12(2), 1985.

Unemployment, real wages and aggregate demand in Europe, Japan and the US. *Carnegie-Rochester Conference Series on Public Policy*, 23, Autumn 1985 (with R. Layard).

Unemployment benefits revisited. *Economic Journal*, June 1985 (with W. Narendranathan and J. Stern).

Error correction, partial adjustment and all that: an expository note. *Oxford Bulletin of Economics and Statistics*, May 1985.

The causes of British unemployment. *National Institute Economic Review*, February 1985 (with R. Layard).

Unemployment insurance and wages. *The Geneva Papers on Risk and Insurance*, January 1985.

Individual earnings in the US. Another look at unionization, schooling, sickness and unemployment using PSID data. *Journal of Labor Economics*, January 1985 (with G. Chowdhury).

The modelling of wages and employment. In D. F. Hendry and K. F. Wallis (eds), *Econometrics and Quantitative Economics*, Blackwell, 1984.

An investigation of the determinants of manufacturing employment in the UK. *Review of Economic Studies*, October 1984.

The estimation of vintage production models in UK manufacturing. *Swedish Journal of Economics*, 85, 1983 (with G. Mizon).

Unions, real wages and employment in Britain 1951–79. *Oxford Economic Papers*, November 1983 (with M. Andrews).

Occupational mobility in Great Britain. *Research in Labor Economics*, 5, 1982 (with D. Metcalf).

Unemployment in the United Kingdom since the war. *Review of Economic Studies*, October 1982 (with M. Andrews).

The determinants of equilibrium unemployment in Britain. *Economic Journal*, September 1982.

Still searching for an explanation of unemployment in interwar Britain. *Journal of Political Economy*, April 1982 (with D. Metcalf and N. Floros).

Wages and unemployment: a general framework. *Economic Journal*, March 1982.

The determinants of occupational success in Britain. *Review of Economic Studies*, January 1982.

Biases in dynamic models with fixed effects. *Econometrica*, November 1981.

The analysis of re-employment probabilities for the unemployed. *Journal of the Royal Statistical Society*, Series A, 143, Part 2, 1980 (with Tony Lancaster).

A picture of male unemployment in Britain. *Economic Journal*, December 1980.

The case for subsidising extra jobs. *Economic Journal*, March 1980 (with R. Layard).

Unemployment and the structure of labour costs. In the Carnegie-Rochester Public Policy Conference Series, No. 11, published as a supplement to the *Journal of Monetary Economics*, 1979.

The effect of collective bargaining on wages. In A. Shorrocks and W. Krelle (eds), *The Economics of Income Distribution*, North-Holland, 1979 (with R. Layard and D. Metcalf).

Education and lifetime patterns of unemployment. *Journal of Political Economy*, October (Part II), 1979.

Estimating the probability of leaving unemployment. *Econometrica*, September 1979.

The effect of unemployment and related benefits on the duration of unemployment. *Economic Journal*, March 1979.

*The Investment Decisions of Firms.* Cambridge Economic Handbooks Series, Cambridge University Press, 1978.

Fixed costs, employment and labour demand over the cycle. *Economica*, November 1978.

The effect of collective bargaining on relative and absolute wages. *British Journal of Industrial Relations*, November 1978 (with R. Layard and D. Metcalf).

Monopolistic industries and monopoly profits. *Economic Journal*, June 1978 (with D. Metcalf).

The plain man's guide to the out-of-work. In *Selected Evidence Submitted to the Royal Commission for Report No. 6: Lower Incomes*, HMSO, May 1978 (with D. Metcalf).

The relationship between the tax structure, financial policy and the rate of investment of the firm. In M. Artis and R. Nobay (eds), *Studies in Modern Economic Analysis*, Macmillan, 1977.

Trade unions and the position of women in the industrial wage structure. *The British Journal of Industrial Relations*, July 1977.

Uncertainty and lags in the investment decisions of firms. *Review of Economic Studies*, June 1977.

The influence of uncertainty on investment. *Economic Journal*, March 1977.

The structure of hours and earnings in British manufacturing industry. *Oxford Economic Papers*, July 1976 (with D. Metcalf and R. Richardson).

On the properties of linear decision rules and their derivation by an iterative procedure. *Econometrica*, March 1976 (with J. Tymes).

Wage structures and quit rates. *International Economic Review*, February 1976.

A closer look at replacement investment. *Journal of Economic Theory*, February 1975.

On expectations, government policy and the rate of investment. *Economica*, August 1974.

On the role of expectations in the pure theory of investment. *The Review of Economic Studies*, January 1974.

# Index